CW00688555

Other Books by the Author

In Search of a Fulfilling Career
Intercepted Signs—Environment Vs. Destiny

Books Co-authored with Jinni Meyer

The Digested Astrologer
When Your Sun Returns
The Spiral of Life

A Journey Through the Birth Chart

Joanne Wickenburg

CRCS PUBLICATIONS
Post Office Box 20850
Reno, Nevada 89515
U.S.A.

Library of Congress Cataloging in Publication Data

Wickenburg, Joanne, 1944-
A journey through the birth chart.

1. Astrology. I. Title.
BF1708.1.W5 1985 133.5 85-7821
ISBN 0-916360-21-0 (pbk.)

INTERNATIONAL STANDARD BOOK NUMBER: 0-916360-21-0
LIBRARY OF CONGRESS CATALOG CARD NUMBER: 85-7821
Published simultaneously in the United States and Canada by:
CRCS Publications
Distributed in the United States and internationally by
CRCS Publications
(Write for current list of worldwide distributors.)

This book is
dedicated
to my children

KIM and GREG WICKENBURG

with all my love!

"There are pioneer
souls
that blaze their paths
where highways never ran."
—Sam Walter Foss

Contents

Author's Note

This book is not a quick reference guide, but a textbook for the serious student of astrology. The material provided has been introduced in much the same format used in a classroom environment. The data available in each chapter and section of each chapter can be applied directly to your own chart as you go along. For this reason, if you don't yet have a copy of your horoscope, it is advisable to have one charted and refer to it as you read.*

If you are a beginning student, please do not jump from chapter to chapter as you might with other books. It is important that you read from beginning to end, in that order, to understand the cyclic unfoldment of signs, houses and planets.

This volume is written mainly for the beginning and intermediate student in hopes that it will help you grasp the very important BASICS that stand behind the more technical aspects of astrology. It has been my experience that these basics are often overlooked in the initial excitement of learning astrology. Therefore, it is my goal, in this volume, to present an in-depth, comprehensive introduction to astrology through this expedition into the signs, houses and planets.

---

*It would be best for beginners to have a competent astrological practitioner calculate the birth chart and show the reader how to understand the basic symbols and placements in his or her chart. If that is not possible, the reader can obtain an accurate complete birth chart by sending name, address, birth date, place, *and exact time*, along with $4, to Astro-Computing Services; P.O. Box 16430; San Diego, CA 92116. Ask for their simplest and most basic "natal chart" using the traditional planets only.

Using Astrology on Your Life Path

Introduction

Most students agree that the study of astrology seems to place you in a different world, or, at least it gives you a totally different perspective of life here on earth. An understanding of our solar system and its effect on human life certainly gives one a greater respect for the vastness and perfect synchronization of the universe, among which our own solar system is only a minute part.

Many people have misconceptions concerning astrology and its application. Basically, astrology helps you to understand better your place in, and relationship to, the world around you. The horoscope, or birth chart, is used as a guide or a road map of life. On your pathway through life you will undoubtedly find roads which are smooth and straight, along with roads having winding curves, deep ruts and upclimbing hills. You may even run into a few dead-end streets along your way. Your birth map can help you to see GRAPHICALLY which streets are best to take at any given time according to the destination you are striving to reach. The road signs are clearly marked within the framework of the chart.

By examining your own horoscope you can see your utmost potentials as well as your greatest handicaps, AND the reasons standing behind both. Yet, while astrology can do all this, IT will not take advantage of the opportunities life offers you. IT will not overcome your limitations, but will point them out and offer guidelines for overcoming them independently. The chart should be used for motivation, for clarification and direction, NOT as an excuse for, or an escape from, living. We can either live up to the potentials described by our charts or take a negative attitude about life and its challenges. Astrology does not negate free will, nor does it alter your heritage, your environment, your religious beliefs or your political leanings. It does, however, help to explain them. Astrology does not foretell the future, but can help you in determining the potential of your future.

The Astronomy of Astrology

Most everyone at one time or another has read an article in a magazine or a newspaper or has read a paperback book describing the twelve different sun-signs. While sun-sign astrology is entertaining and often superficially meaningful, it doesn't take much thought to realize that if we are, for example, everything our sun-signs say we are and nothing more, there would be only twelve different types of people in the world. One out of every twelve people would look alike, think alike, talk alike, have identical beliefs and so on. The fact is, no two people are alike and no two birth charts are either. It is erroneous to categorize people into twelve such specific types or personalities. The sun-sign does, however, have a very important function in the astrological chart, just as each planet and sign plays an important role in the development of personality. The sun-sign is only one of many factors which make up the total birth chart.

EACH CHART CONTAINS ALL TWELVE SIGNS and houses, along with the Sun, the Moon and planets, each in a different relationship to all others. This explains why each of us function differently in the various outer areas of life. For example, you project one personality while at work, another when at play. Your children see you differently from your friends. On the other hand, your friends know you to be someone different from the person your parents would describe.

While it is not the purpose of this volume to go into the mathematical calculations involved with chart construction, it is important for you to understand from the very beginning of your studies the basic structure from which a horoscope is derived. The birth chart is a map of our solar system as it was on the date, at the time and from the place of birth, as seen from the earth's point of view. As you were born on the earth rather than the sun you must work with the GEOCENTRIC, or earth-centered, longitudes of the planets rather than the HELIOCENTRIC, or sun-centered, positions and build the chart mathematically around this concept.

Realize that the planets are, in reality, orbiting the Sun. However, while standing on the surface of the earth, held down by its gravity, it APPEARS that the planets, the Sun and Moon, are moving around us, as we are not sensually aware of the motion of our own planet. As we spin around in space, making one complete rotation every 24 hours and taking one calendar year to orbit the Sun, we look up in the sky and see the Sun, Moon and planets passing overhead. It is their positions in relation to the place and time of birth with which we will be working.

Maybe it's a lesson in humility to realize that we on earth are not the center of the universe. Yet, we are a RESULT of our universe and that result can be seen in the relationship of the other planets to our planet, earth. Astrologers feel that this relationship plays a part in defining the particular destiny of each individual creation on our planet. You might say, we are bringing the laws of the universe down to earth to find how the cosmic pattern affects life hereon. Therefore, we make our mathematical calculations according to the birth locality and consider it to be the center of our individualized universe.

The geocentric and heliocentric patterns are illustrated on the following page. Notice that glyphs have been used for the planets. If you have not yet memorized these glyphs, you will need to do so in order to recognize them in charts and astrological reference books.

There are two systems used in astrology. These are the tropical and sidereal zodiacs. Tropical astrology is far more widely used in the western hemisphere. Because of its popularity, greater acceptance and relatability to our culture, the information in this book will be geared to the tropical system.

The sidereal zodiac is based, abstractly, on the constellations. Constellations are separate groupings of stars extending far beyond our solar system. They are so distant, in fact, that they can be measured only in light years. Because of their great distance from the earth, most astrologers feel that they do not have as strong an influence on human life as do the tropical signs which are derived from the ecliptic, or Sun's

HELIOCENTRIC (Sun-centered)

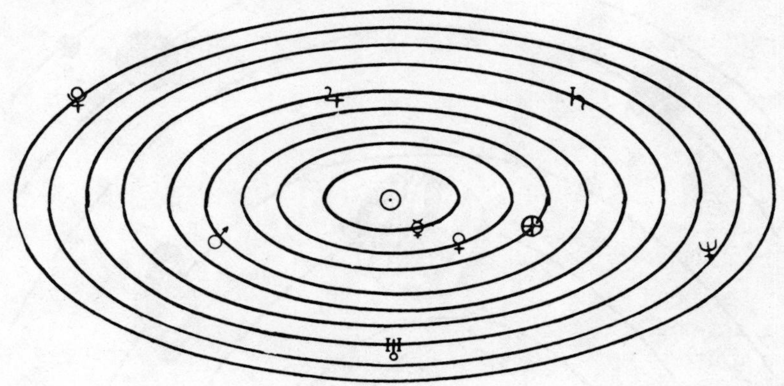

GEOCENTRIC (earth-centered)

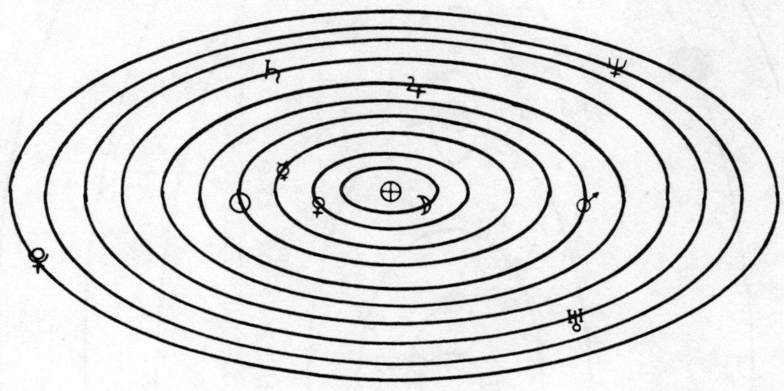

(☉) Sun (⊕) Earth (☽) Moon

(☿) Mercury (♀) Venus (♂) Mars

(♃) Jupiter (♄) Saturn (♅) Uranus

(♆) Neptune (♇) Pluto

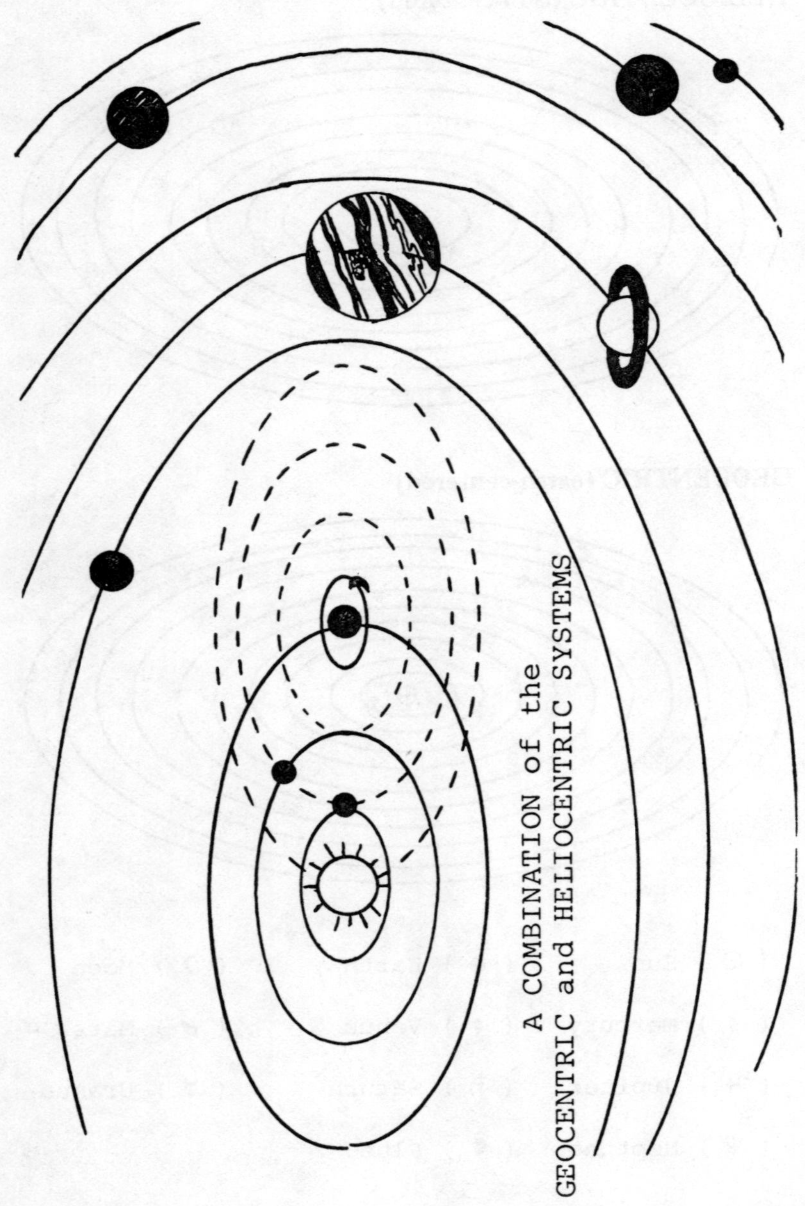
A COMBINATION of the
GEOCENTRIC and HELIOCENTRIC SYSTEMS

apparent pathway around the earth. Even though each constellation covers a different number of degrees of space, sidereal astrologers use the circle they create and divide it into equal 30 degree segments to represent the sidereal signs. Due to the very slow movement of the stars in the constellations, the sidereal zodiac is a moving one, while the tropical zodiac is fixed. At this time in history, the two zodiacs are approximately one full sign apart.

While some 1st magnitude stars are used in chart interpretation, their influences are not as strong as those of the planets. Unlike the star constellations, planets are close enough to the earth that their distance can be measured in miles. Astrologers believe that the planets' geocentric (earth centered) orbits build energy fields which are collected and vitalized by the solar energy. As the Sun appears to move around the earth, it distributes this energy.

In tropical astrology, the ecliptic (the Sun's apparent pathway around the earth) is divided into 12 sections of 30 degrees each. These sections have been given astrological names—Aries, Taurus, Gemini, Cancer, Leo, Virgo, Libra, Scorpio, Sagittarius, Capricorn, Aquarius and Pisces—not to be confused with the star groupings, or constellations, carrying the same names (see illustration on page 8).

As the sun moves through these 30 degree sections (signs), our four yearly seasons are experienced. Therefore, the tropical zodiac has become the foundation of our current calendar. The first day of spring each year begins when the ecliptic and celestial equator (the earth's equator as it would be if extended out into space) cross. This marks the first degree of our first astrological sign, Aries. As you can see in the illustration on page 9, spring and summer are experienced when the Sun is moving through the northern hemisphere while autumn and winter are experienced when it moves through the southern hemisphere.

It is from the seasonal changes, brought on by this phenomenon that astrologers, at the very beginning of time, began to take note and record correlating human characteristics and actions.

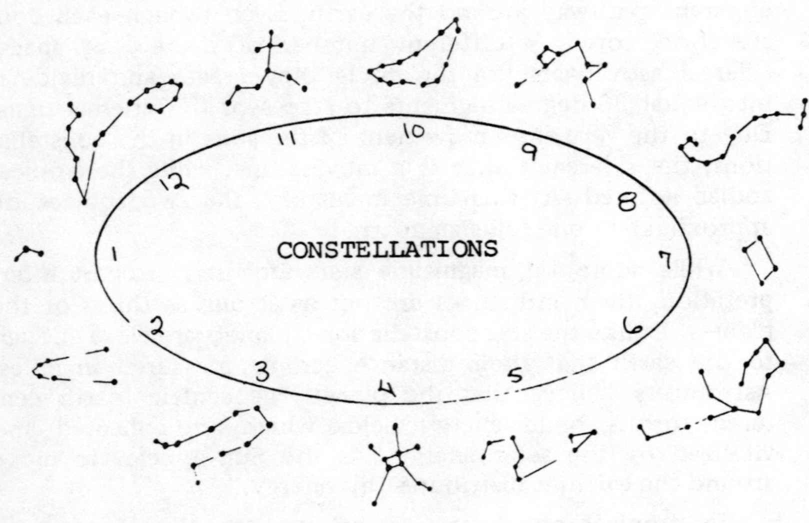

1. Aries
2. Taurus
3. Gemini
4. Cancer
5. Leo
6. Virgo
7. Libra
8. Scorpio
9. Sagittarius
10. Capricorn
11. Aquarius
12. Pisces

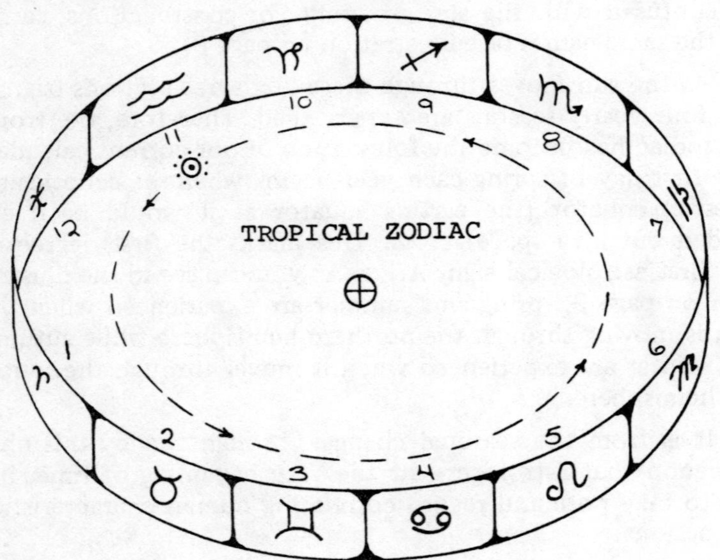

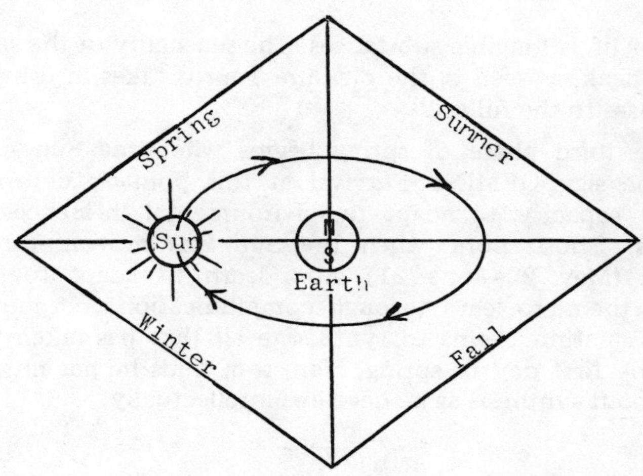

The Seasons as the Basis of the Tropical Zodiac

Spring

The beginning of spring marks a period of new birth. Animals come out of hybernation; mating season begins. Seeds are planted for future crops. The world takes on a new lightness after its winter rest. Similarly, those born when the Sun was moving through the sign ARIES (March 21 - April 20) are the pioneers of our world. These people, while not always having a clear vision of what the future might bring, must meet the challenge to move toward it with courage. Instincts are strong in their search for selfhood.

From Aries, the Sun moves into TAURUS where the energy of spring is concentrated. Seeds begin to take root. Conception has taken place in the animal world. The results are soon to be seen. Spring is at its midpoint and both man and nature are concerned with what will manifest from the activities initiated during the first 30 day interval. People born when the Sun was moving through Taurus (April 21 - May 21) display this concern for getting results in various ways. Often, they attach themselves to the material world or the physical pleasures life has to offer. Others are acutely aware of the value of life's tangible substances. The sensuality of the season is at a peak, as seen in the pleasure Taurus takes in using the five senses to the fullest.

The third phase of spring begins when the Sun moves into the sign GEMINI. Survival at this point is dependent on the capacity to adapt to environmental influences and changes. Those born when the Sun was moving through Gemini (May 22–June 21) must learn to adapt to those around them, to learn through communication and cooperation. As nature begins to synthesize all that has taken place since the first day of spring, man, too, finds he has much to learn about synthesis as he develops intellectually.

Summer

Mother nature is busy nurturing all that she has born. And so, man's nurturing instincts are developed. The warmth of summer manifests through the sensitivity and warmth of character displayed in the CANCER born individual (June 22–July 22). Maternal instincts run strong. Just as animals are prepared to protect their young, so Cancer individuals protect all that is near to them.

In mid-summer, the Sun moves toward LEO and all of nature is in full bloom. Infant animals are at play; life is for enjoying. The purpose of all that has gone before becomes evident in the splendor of a beautiful summer day. Likewise, it is shown through the confidence displayed by the Leo-born individual (July 23–August 23). The radiant personality reminds us all that this person was born at a time when nature was most generous.

Soon the world again is at a point of transition. This is evident in the VIRGO phase of summer. A time of reaping what has been sown is right around the corner and preparation must begin. Work is the keynote here. The person born during this phase (August 24–September 23) is concerned with the responsibilities and realities at hand.

Fall

Autumn is here before we know it. Leaves begin to turn color. Man and nature must now work together in harmony in order to maintain balance. Crops are ready to be reaped. Man sees, objectively, the products he has created and realizes it could never have been without the help of Mother Nature herself. He learns, then, cooperation and balance in all things, be it concerning his relationship with nature or his relationship to his fellow man. As leaves blend in harmonious hues, those born when the Sun was in LIBRA (September 24-October 23) learn to do likewise. Balance and justice become the ultimate goal.

As the Sun enters SCORPIO, leaves begin falling from the trees. Petals of flowers have dried and returned to the earth. The more delicate of nature's creations die while those stronger survive even though the elements have taken their toll. Nature begins the process of regeneration, just as individuals born during the Sun's transit through Scorpio (October 24-November 22) experience the depth of life and are acutely aware of mortality. Dissatisfied with the superficial, these people search for a deeper meaning to their lives.

In the last month of autumn, the Sun moves into SAGITTARIUS. It is now time to seek out the remnants of nature's gifts and store them for the coming winter. Survival now depends on foresight and vision. Those born at this phase of the seasonal cycle (November 23-December 21) have a natural gift for visualizing future possibilities, recognizing that yesterday has come and gone and tomorrow is another day.

Winter

As the Sun enters CAPRICORN, nature takes a rest. The earth is barren and the animal kingdom has found refuge for the winter months. There is an air of austerity. The world is awed by the transition that has taken place. Those born at this time of year (December 22-January 20) project that same austerity and demand respect for their capacity to survive. Just as animals are finding protection from the elements, Capricorn individuals build a wall of protection around their feelings of vulnerability to the environment.

At the midpoint of the season, when the Sun moves into AQUARIUS (January 21-February 19), the air seems electrical. There is a freshness that both cleanses and stimulates.

Electrical energy is so potent now that touching certain objects can literally shock you. And, so can the strength of the Aquarius personality. Intuition strikes like the lightning of the season. Ice crusting over the earth is shattered by the thunder, just as the Aquarius personality has the power to break through barriers which limit creative expression.

The cycle nears its end as the Sun moves into the last zodiacal sign, PISCES. Winter is almost over; spring is almost here. All of nature seems in a state of limbo. Faith is the keynote for survival. Those born when the Sun was moving through Pisces (February 20–March 20) often feel out of step with the rest of the world. No longer do they fit into the patterns that have been, yet they remain unable to open the gates to what lies ahead. Just as Mother Nature is making a commitment to start anew, those born under the sign of Pisces must commit their lives to some future cause having some greater than personal significance. Then, before you know it, spring returns, promises are fulfilled, a new life begins and the cycle renews itself.

* * *

It should be obvious at this point that a pattern has been established as a result of each season's unfoldment. The first month in each season requires initiative, as does the birth of any new cycle. The signs ruling each season's FIRST MONTH are called CARDINAL. During the second month of each season, energy is concentrated. The more tangible results of the season's purpose manifest at this midpoint. The signs ruling these seasonal MIDPOINTS are called FIXED. The last month in each season requires adjustment from one season to the requirements and needs of the next. Both nature and man are being tested for adaptability. The signs ruling the third or LAST MONTH in each season are called MUTABLE or COMMON.

The Cardinal, Fixed and Mutable signs make up the . . .

Qualities as Modes of Action

When converting the seasonal changes into human behavior patterns we find:

CARDINAL SIGNS (Aries, Cancer, Libra, Capricorn) represent the basic search for selfhood. ARIES describes the need to define yourself as separate from others through independent activity. CANCER represents the need to build foundations which provide that identity with security and a sense of belongingness. LIBRA represents the need to meet others in a sharing experience in order to develop the "relative identity," and CAPRICORN describes the need to establish yourself at a social level, thereby developing a social identity.

FIXED SIGNS (Taurus, Leo, Scorpio, Aquarius) correspond to each season's midpoint where endurance becomes an issue. For this reason, fixed signs describe a need for stability, perseverance and resourcefulness in order to maintain the identity requirements of the Cardinal signs. TAURUS represents the need to sustain and maintain the Aries-identity by acquiring the substances necessary for survival. LEO maintains the emotional equilibrium of Cancer by offering outlets for self-expression and a sense of purpose. SCORPIO maintains Libra's relative identity by regenerating selfish motives. AQUARIUS maintains the social identity of Capricorn by offering originality and insight into human needs and progressive potentials.

MUTABLE SIGNS (Gemini, Virgo, Sagittarius, Pisces) correspond to the transitional periods of our seasons when adaptability is required. For this reason, mutable signs are associated with mental development and adaptation from old patterns into new modes of living. GEMINI represents the need to collect information from a variety of sources. In VIRGO, the information is classified, digested and put to some useful application. SAGITTARIUS offers the capacity to see potentials of the future, and PISCES encourages us to recognize and have faith in the unknown.

Elements as Temperament

Signs can also be divided according to the ELEMENTS of Fire, Earth, Air and Water. Elements describe temperamental patterns which are expressed through the activity-mode described by the Qualities. The four signs found in each Quality are each in a different Element, further describing the individual characteristics of the twelve astrological signs.

FIRE SIGNS (Aries, Leo, Sagittarius) are goal oriented and concerned with future opportunities. Often described as inspirational, fire signs, more than all others, show where you need goals. As each sign in the Fire Element is of a different Quality, the mode of action taken to achieve these goals will be different. For example:

ARIES (Cardinal/Fire) Initiates action according to future goals.

LEO (Fixed/Fire) Views the future with fixity of purpose.

SAGITTARIUS (Mutable/Fire) Adapts mentally in order to pursue the future optimistically.

EARTH SIGNS (Taurus, Virgo, Capricorn), on the other hand, are concerned with matters of the here and now. They build practical substances which support inspiration. With earth, you are challenged to keep your feet planted on the ground. You need to analyze experience to ascertain its potential worth. Earth signs always follow Fire, assisting each of us in making real what begins as only an ideal. As each sign in the Earth Element falls into a different Quality, the mode of action taken to achieve these results will be different. For example:

TAURUS (Fixed/Earth) Needs to get results for efforts expended.

VIRGO (Mutable/Earth) Needs to get results by using knowledge productively.

CAPRICORN (Cardinal/Earth) Needs to get results through use of ambition at a social level.

AIR SIGNS (Gemini, Libra, Aquarius) deal with the development of objectivity which comes from relating and communicating with others. Here, you learn by sharing experiences and listening to the feedback offered as a result of the sharing. The Air Element provides the basis from which curiosity is aroused and the vehicles through which communication takes place. Information is acquired at the level, or through the mode of action, described by the Qualities. For example:

GEMINI (Mutable/Air) Needs to gain knowledge through a variety of mental experiences.

LIBRA (Cardinal/Air) Needs to gain knowledge through interaction with others, particularly one-to-one.

AQUARIUS (Fixed/Air) Needs to gain and solidify knowledge through social experiences and group experiments.

WATER SIGNS (Cancer, Scorpio, Pisces) While Fire signs are concerned with the future, the Water Element is at home with the past. Being emotional in temperament, Water signs operate on the basis of feeling rather than logic. The emotional responses aroused through Water activity are based on past experiences which are stored at various levels of the subconscious. The memories strongly affect your daily life. As each of the Water signs fall into a different Quality, access to those memories is qualified. For example:

CANCER (Cardinal/Water) Recallable memories affecting present security.

SCORPIO (Fixed/Water) Repressed memories needing regeneration.

PISCES (Mutable/Water) Collective memories beyond personal experience only.

Genders

Another type of sign division is seen in the GENDERS. All Earth and Water signs are FEMININE, while all FIRE and AIR signs are MASCULINE. Masculine signs describe the need for outward, assertive activity, relating to the positive electrical current. Feminine signs are receptive, attracting experiences rather than initiating them independently.

At one time, genders were referred to as "positive" (masculine) and "negative" (feminine). Fortunately, these terms are now becoming obsolete because of the tendency for the beginning student to misinterpret the wording. "Positive" infers energy out-put, while "negative" infers energy-receiving. The connotation of good and bad does not apply to the sign genders. Since the feminist movement, terms such as "assertive" (rather than "masculine") and "receptive" (rather than "feminine") might be better statements for the genders in order to avoid any sexual connotation concerning their expression.

The Houses

While signs describe specific personality characteristics and needs, houses show the outer areas of life through which the signs seek expression and development. Houses have no personality traits. They describe environmental experiences available to everyone. The signs and planets, as they are distributed throughout the house structure, show your individual attitudes toward, and needs regarding, these external departments of life. Each house will be found in the same area of all charts you see. Houses only become personally meaningful once the signs and planets have been included.

There is a similarity between the chart divisions (houses) and a dial of a clock which separates the hours of our day. In fact, the TIME of day in which a birth takes place determines where the signs are located in the horoscope. To understand

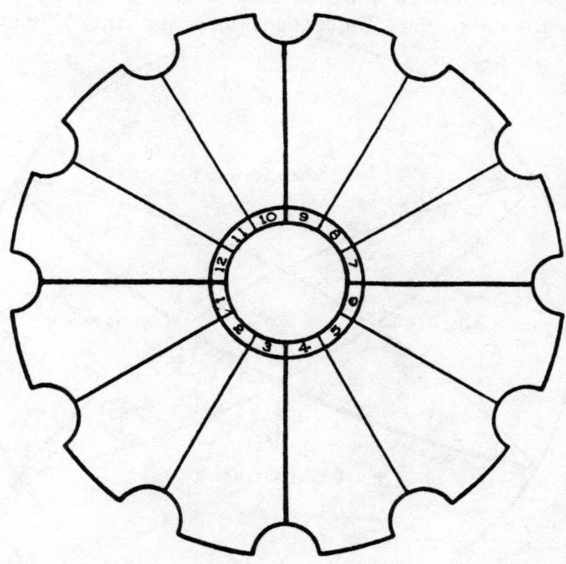

Illustration #1

fully the interpretive significance of the houses you should first consider how they are derived. To construct a chart, an astrologer must obtain the client's date, time and place of birth. From the recorded birth information, he or she makes a map of the heavens as they were at that time and from that place by calculating to find the placement of the signs and planets in relation to that space. Notice in Illustration #1 that the houses are numbered toward the center of the wheel. The house CUSPS are the lines dividing each house, or section.

There are two major divisions on all charts—the horizon and the meridian. The horizon divides the chart horizontally. The SIGN through which the horizon passes, when extended out to the east beyond the earth to meet the ecliptic (the Sun's apparent pathway around the earth) is called the Ascendant, or Rising Sign. This will become the sign on the 1st house cusp of the birth chart. See Illustration #2.

(Notice, in the illustration below, that arrows are pointing from the points where the horizon and meridian meet the ecliptic. These points determine the Ascendant/Descendant axis and the Midheaven/Nadir axis.)

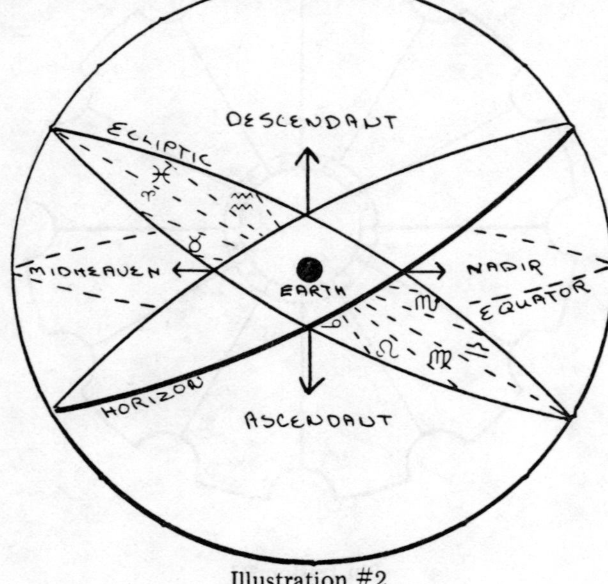

Illustration #2

The western intersection is the Descendant, or setting point. The sign through which the horizon passes, when extended out to the west determines what sign will occupy the 7th house cusp of the birth chart. The Ascendant and Descendant signs will differ in each chart, as they can only be determined from the combination of the birth date, time and place.

The meridian divides the chart vertically. It is mathematically found from the point on the ecliptic most highly elevated at the time of birth. This vertical division creates the Midheaven (the sign on the 10th house cusp) and the Nadir (4th house cusp). The major divisions caused by the horizon and meridian cut the chart into four sections called "quadrants." See Illustrations # 3, 4, and 5.

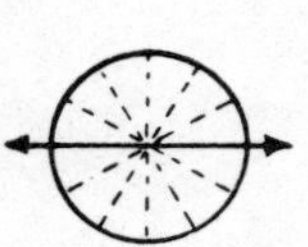

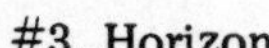

#3. Horizon

#4. Meridian

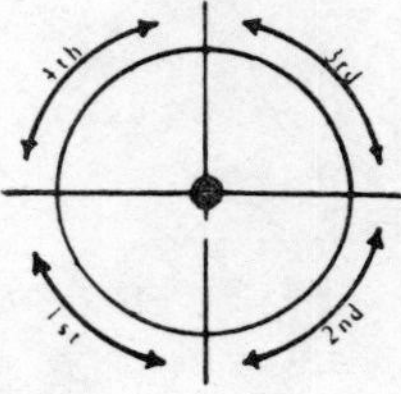

#5. Quadrants

Each of the 12 houses rule an approximate two hour period, equaling a total of 24 hours, relating to the time it takes the earth to make one full rotation, or for us to experience one calendar day. The houses on the upper half of the chart, or above the horizon, rule the daytime hours, while the houses below the horizon rule the nighttime. In other words, if you were born during the night, your Sun sign (the sign through which the Sun was moving when you were born) would be found below the horizon of your chart, somewhere between the 1st and 7th houses. If you were born at noon it would be located near the 10th house cusp, or Midheaven. See Illustration # 6.

Houses begin numerically at the eastern horizon, or the extreme left side of the wheel. Due to the rotation of the earth, any sign could appear on any house cusp over a 24-

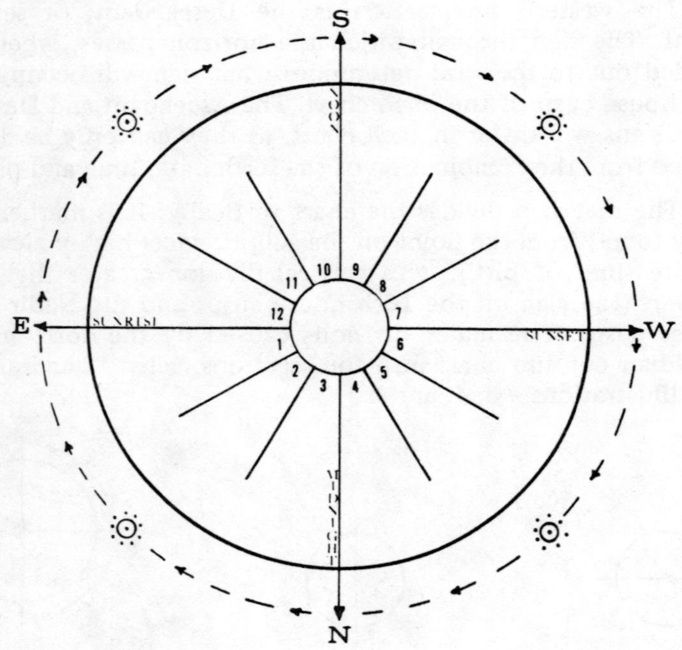

#6. The Astrological Clock

hour period of time. For this reason, the time of birth is of extreme importance in the construction of an accurate horoscope.

Before going on to describe the meanings of the houses, it is important to restate the interpretive significance of the houses apart from the signs and planets. SIGNS describe personal NEEDS and the ATTITUDES that result from those needs. HOUSES, on the other hand, deal with EXTERNAL AFFAIRS, describing AREAS OF LIFE through which the needs and attitudes of the signs are expressed and experienced. Houses show NO personality characteristics. SIGNS ON HOUSES describe your approach to the various areas of your life. PLANETS IN HOUSES describe the ACTIVITIES taking place. Once this basic principle is established, the chart interpretation becomes more concrete.

First House

The DOOR TO LIFE. The first house literally provides a doorway to a life outside yourself. Here, you meet new experiences which shape your self concepts. The SIGN on its cusp, called the Ascendant, or Rising Sign, describes the mask you wear when meeting the world. Through your first house involvements you develop your self-image. The sign on its cusp describes how you project yourself to others based on this image. Therefore, the Ascendant sign describes how others see you, your mannerisms, appearance and a quality needed to build self confidence.

As houses rule external fields of activity only, your particular orientation toward these experiences can be described only by the sign on the cusps. The first house, in itself, offers an opportunity to LIVE in the outer world—to become an independent individual among others. Your particular way of approaching life is described by the sign found on the cusp.

Second House

The DOOR TO SURVIVAL. The second house rules all personal assets or resources. These are the resources required for survival. Here, you find your income (not including finances provided by others which you have not personally earned). The strengths you develop, not only from a material level, but psychological, physical and spiritual strengths, are also ruled by the 2nd house of your chart. The SIGN on the 2nd house cusp describes the type of strength needed for survival along with defining your general attitude toward, and use of, material assets. Through the experiences provided by the 2nd house, you develop values, self worth and psychological strength.

Third House

The DOOR TO KNOWLEDGE. The third house deals with environmental experiences which shape your mentality and understanding of concrete facts. It rules the immediate surroundings, the neighborhood, community and relationships with siblings. All short distance travel and communications which encourage learning fall into its domain. In essence, the third house deals with those experiences which teach you to cooperate with others in a community sense. The SIGN on the third house cusp describes how you learn through and relate to environmental contacts—whether they be in your community, with neighbors or relatives. As the third house rules the educational facilities in the environment, the sign on its cusp describes your basic orientation toward learning.

Fourth House

The DOOR TO YOUR HOME. The fourth house rules the home and the parent in the home which played the strongest role in shaping your emotional foundations. Located at the bottom of the chart, this house deals literally with the security base you stand upon. It deals with your heritage, family involvements and due to its rulership over the home, it rules all real estate and property investments. The SIGN on the fourth house cusp describes your needs concerning family living. It characterizes the inner feelings you have about yourself based on early home experiences.

Fifth House

The DOOR TO REPRODUCTION. The fifth house rules all creative experiences and expressions which help you to maintain security by offering creative outlets for emotion. Here is the house of recreation, creativity, play, love and children. In the fifth house you find opportunity to see yourself reflected through your creations, be they your offspring or your works of art. This house defines, by sign, your legacy, or what part of yourself that will continue to exist even after your physical life is over. The SIGN on the fifth house cusp describes your approach to creative activity as well as how you deal with rearing children. It also suggests personal needs regarding romantic involvements which help you to outwardly express your emotions.

Sixth House

The DOOR TO RESPONSIBILITY. In the sixth house you confront responsibilities which require routine consideration. These responsibilities include those you confront on a daily basis at work as well as responsibilities involving your health and physical body. Through your sixth house activities, you learn to make the personal adjustments necessary to handle daily crises. The SIGN on your sixth house cusp describes your basic needs within (and therefore your general approach to) the daily routine of your job. It also points to a part of your body, or bodily functioning, that requires your attention in order to maintain good health.

The first six houses deal with experiences which encourage personal development. The last six houses rule experiences involving others.

Seventh House

The DOOR TO RELATIONSHIPS. The seventh house rules all relationships which involve give and take. This is the house of marriage and/or partnerships which require co-operation and sharing. The sign on the seventh house describes the type of feedback you need from others to gain objectivity concerning your own self projection. It describes how you see yourself reflected through others, therefore defining a quality you need in a mate to complement your own life direction. In essence, the seventh house rules your "other half."

Eighth House

The DOOR TO REGENERATION. The eighth house deals with the changes that are necessary in order to maintain relationships with others. Here, personal sacrifices are made in order to contribute to joint causes. The eighth house involves the death of substances or attitudes which have outlived their usefulness. To some degree, it rules the actual death of the body. However, astrology, in itself, cannot predict when death will occur, but only when CHANGES must be made. This house also rules taxes, as the payment of taxes is necessary to maintain our position as a member of society. The SIGN on the eighth house describes how you approach life's changes. It also defines an attitude that must be regenerated (inferring that at first the negative quality of the sign is evident) in order to maintain relationships over a long period of time.

Ninth House

The DOOR TO WISDOM. The ninth house experience offers an opportunity to expand mentally beyond the limits of the immediate environment. Here, you find travel opportunity, higher education and religious, or philosophical training. In the ninth house you learn about principles and ethical standards. Through the experiences attracted here, you acquire a broader point of view. The SIGN on the ninth house cusp describes your approach to religious experiences and your most basic philosophical needs. It also defines your approach to higher learning, be it through extended education or through travel and learning of different cultures. Here, in the ninth house, you meet experiences that are, at first, "foreign" to you.

Tenth House

The DOOR TO SUCCESS. The tenth house rules your public reputation and all those things that go into its development. Here, you find the career, along with the parent in your life who most strongly affected your public image. The SIGN on the tenth house cusp describes your needs in reference to a profession. It defines how others see you when functioning as a professional. This is your social image or "name." The sign describes a quality you need to project through social involvements in order to feel successful and to establish social foundations.

Eleventh House

The DOOR TO THE FUTURE. Through eleventh house activities you begin to define goals for your future. Here, you look ahead to find what tomorrow might bring and you discover the choices available to you in terms of progress. The eleventh house rules all associations and friendships which encourage or help you to formulate goals for your future. As it rules group activities, conventions and social experiences in general, the eleventh house shows where sharing at a group level leads to awareness of future possibilities. The SIGN on the eleventh house cusp describes how you approach social experiences and the types of people to whom you are attracted as a friend. It describes how you view progress and how you

The Houses as Areas of Life

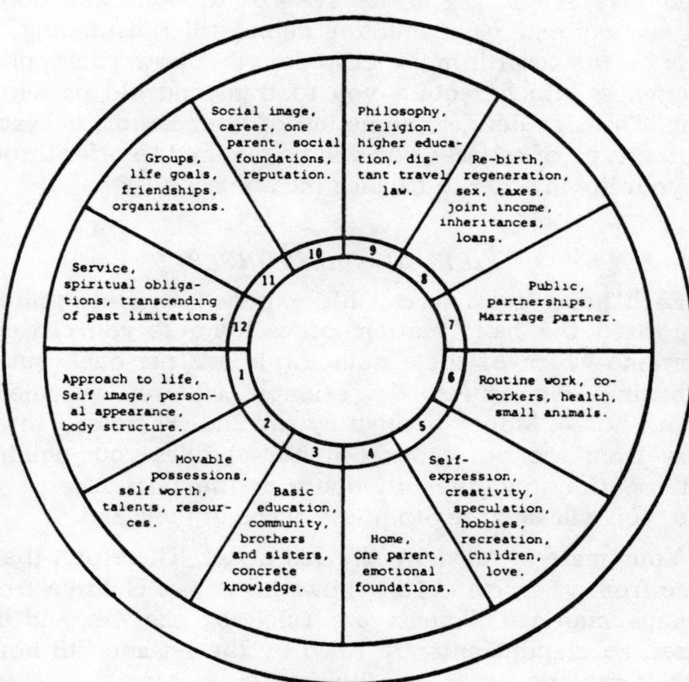

go about building a new tomorrow. Your approach to humanitarian causes and the needs you have regarding such activities are described by the sign on this cusp.

Twelfth House

The DOOR TO THE UNCONSCIOUS. Found within the experiences of this house is an accumulation of all past experiences which lie hidden in the unconscious. This is the house of "karma," where you meet tests which challenge your faith. Ruling institutions of all types, the twelfth house provides opportunities to make restitution for past errors in preparation for future living. Unconscious motives must be confronted here in the last house of the chart.

The twelfth house rules all that stands behind you, either to offer support and inner strength, or problems which continually trip you. The law of cause and effect (karma) experienced here refers to spiritual rewards for jobs well done as well as required payments for debts still outstanding. The SIGN on the twelfth house cusp describes how you approach experiences which require you to transcend old patterns of living. This sign defines the nature of your karmic obligations and the type of services you will be required to offer throughout your life in order to balance the books.

Derivative Houses

Each house rules several life experiences. Once you have memorized the basic matters of each house you can easily determine which of these houses rule less personal, but still interesting, experiences. For example, children are ruled by the 5th house. Money is ruled by the 2nd. Therefore, the 2nd house from the 5th (your 6th house) rules your childrens' earnings. Counting the 5th house as the 1st house of your child, you will find the 6th house becomes their 2nd.

Your mate is ruled by the 7th house. Therefore, the 5th house from your 7th (11th) shows his or her children from a previous marriage. Parents are ruled by the 4th and 10th houses, so grandparents are ruled by the 1st and 7th houses, as they are the 4th and 10th houses (parents) from those ruling your folks. Brothers and sisters are ruled by the 3rd house. Their partners can be found in your 9th house, as it is house number 7 from that ruling siblings.

The 4th and 10th houses rule parents. By looking to your 8th and 2nd houses you can see their viewpoint of you, as these are the 5th houses from the 4th and 10th. The parent represented by your 10th house sees you as the sign on your 2nd house cusp. The parent ruled by your 4th house views you as the sign on your 8th house cusp. Both parents do not see you in the same light, nor do they see you as others do. What is it about your personality that stands out in THEIR eyes? Aunts and uncles are ruled by the 6th and 12th houses of your chart, as these houses are in a 3rd house relationship (brothers and sisters) to those ruling your parents.

Based on this theory, you can determine the earning potential of your business in the 11th house of the chart. It is the 2nd house (finances) from the 10th. The money you TAKE HOME, however, is shown in your own 2nd house.

Using derivative houses can be fascinating and fun. This technique enables you to locate any individual or any matter having any affect on your life. As a matter of fact, you can look at your chart to find the different characteristics expressed through each of your children. Rather than focussing on the 5th house only to represent children, consider the 5th house to describe your approach to raising children and to characterize important qualities about your first child. The 2nd child will be described by the 7th house sign, as it is the 3rd house from the 5th (the brother or sister of your 1st child). The 9th house describes the 3rd child, as it is the brother or sister of the 2nd child (7th) and so on around the wheel. It is amazing how much information can be obtained by using derivative houses.

Houses and the Qualities

Houses and signs which correspond numerically (Aries/ 1st house, Taurus/2nd house, Gemini/3rd house, Cancer/4th house, etc.) have a strong relationship with each other, even though the signs may not occupy those same house cusps in an actual birth chart. While it is still early to grasp the full significance of the relationship between signs and their "natural" houses, consider the following information. If you find it difficult to assimilate now, don't worry. This relationship will be discussed again later in the book, at which time you might want to review the following material.

Cardinal Signs/Angular Houses

Just as signs are divided into Qualities and Elements, houses can be similarly categorized. The houses corresponding numerically to the Cardinal signs are called ANGULAR. These houses (1, 4, 7, 10) deal with outer activities which build character and ultimately develop the self image at both a personal and social level. For example:

ARIES: The house on which you find Aries shows where you need to know you are an independent entity, capable of functioning on your own, while the . . .

1ST HOUSE sign describes you as you meet the outside world. This sign describes your mannerisms and general approach to new experiences.

CANCER: The house on which you find Cancer shows where you need to build boundaries around activity in order to find security, while the . . .

4TH HOUSE sign describes your home and family involvements which qualify security. It defines your approach to security matters.

LIBRA: The house on which you find Libra shows where you need to share with others on a one to one basis, to develop objectivity and learn cooperation, while the . . .

7TH HOUSE sign describes the people in your life with whom you share and must cooperate.

CAPRICORN: The house on which you find Capricorn shows where you need to find security within the social structure and establish a sense of social belongingness, while the . . .

10TH HOUSE sign describes your professional involvements and a quality for which you are socially recognized.

Fixed Signs/Succedent Houses

Houses corresponding numerically to the fixed signs (2, 5, 8, 11) are called SUCCEDENT. These houses deal with outer experiences requiring perseverance and maintenance in order to sustain life. For example:

TAURUS: The house on which you find Taurus describes where you need to develop a practical outlook on life and obtain practical results for efforts expended, while the . . .

2ND HOUSE sign describes experiences providing tangible substances and qualities needing developing in order to maintain life.

LEO: The house on which you find Leo describes where you need to find self expression which develops confidence and self-importance, to make life purposeful, while the . . .

5TH HOUSE sign describes experiences demonstrating your importance and the legacy you leave through children or creative works.

SCORPIO: The house on which you find Scorpio shows where you need to regenerate selfish motives and unite with others in an intense experience, while the . . .

8TH HOUSE sign defines the changes experienced as a result of involvement with others. Here, you find your approach to life changes.

AQUARIUS: The house on which you find Aquarius describes where you need to look beyond fact and structure, to seek out experiences which induce progress, while the . . .

11TH HOUSE sign defines experiences involving humanitarian progress and your outlook for the future and its choices.

Mutable Signs/Cadent Houses

Houses corresponding numerically to the MUTABLE signs (3, 6, 9, 12) are called CADENT. Here, life requires that you learn to adjust and develop intellectual skills. For example:

GEMINI: The house on which you find Gemini describes where you need to investigate new ideas and allow natural curiosity freedom to learn through communication, while the . . .

3RD HOUSE sign defines your approach to experiences which provide learning via environmental educational facilities and the communication media.

VIRGO: The house on which you find Virgo describes where you need to analyze, digest and perfect knowledge until it can be used productively at a daily level, while the . . .

6TH HOUSE sign defines your approach to experiences requiring the useful application of knowledge and establishment of routine.

SAGITTARIUS: The house on which you find Sagittarius describes where you need to broaden your horizons, to look ahead and to aim toward long-term goals, while the . . .

9TH HOUSE sign describes your approach to higher education, travel, foreign involvements and concepts and all things which expand consciousness.

PISCES: The house on which you find Pisces describes where you need to understand and have faith in the higher laws of the universe and all that connects you with the past, collectively and personally, while the . . .

12TH HOUSE sign describes your "karmic" obligations and approach to collective service as well as its knowledge.

Houses and the Elements

Houses can also be divided to correspond with the Elements of Fire, Earth, Air and Water. In this division you will find the Houses of Life (1, 5, 9), Houses of Substance (2, 6, 10), Houses of Relationships (3, 7, 11) and the Houses of Endings (4, 8, 12).

Houses of Life/Fire Element

The Houses of Life (1, 5, 9) correspond to the Fire Signs. These houses describe fields of activity encouraging continual development and expression of selfhood. Their relationship to the Fire Signs is described briefly below:

ARIES: Its house shows where you need to be independent, while the . . .

1ST HOUSE sign describes how you project your independent identity to others.

LEO: Its house shows where you need to feel important and purposeful, while the . . .

5TH HOUSE sign describes how your creativity manifests outwardly.

SAGITTARIUS: Its house shows where you need to understand future concepts, while the . . .

9TH HOUSE sign describes how you approach higher learning and religious experiences.

Houses of Substance/Earth Element

The Houses of Substance (2, 6, 10) correspond numerically to the Earth Signs. They describe areas of life encouraging practicality and tangible accomplishments. Their relationship to the Earth Signs is briefly described below:

TAURUS: Its house shows where you need to be practical and down to earth, while the . . .

2ND HOUSE sign describes the practical resources and personal strengths you need to develop.

VIRGO: Its house shows where you need to establish techniques for living, while the . . .

6TH HOUSE sign describes how you approach routine responsibilities.

CAPRICORN: Its house shows where you need to belong within the social structure, while the . . .

10TH HOUSE sign describes your approach to professional matters and the nature of your reputation or social mission.

Houses of Relationships/Air Element

The Houses of Relationships (3, 7, 11) correspond numerically to the Air Signs. They describe areas of life encouraging cooperation with others. The relationship between these signs and houses is described briefly below:

GEMINI: Its house shows where you learn through variety and communication, while the . . .

3RD HOUSE sign describes your approach to environmental learning facilities and contacts.

LIBRA: Its house shows where you need to share with others on a one to one basis, while the . . .

7TH HOUSE sign describes how you deal with interpersonal relationships requiring cooperation.

AQUARIUS: Its house shows where you need to learn to relate intellectually at a group level, acknowledging what is best for the group, rather than each individual within it, while the . . .

11TH HOUSE sign describes the types of groups to which you are attracted and your potential to contribute to them.

Houses of Endings/Water Element

The Houses of Endings (4, 8, 12) correspond numerically to the Water Signs. These houses describe areas of life requiring emotional grounding. Here, the past shows its influence on your sense of emotional well-being. Their relationship to the Water Signs is shown briefly below:

CANCER: Its house shows where you need security and a sense of personal belongingness, while the . . .

4TH HOUSE sign describes your emotional foundations.

SCORPIO: Its house shows where you experience regeneration as a result of intense involvements with others, while the . . .

8TH HOUSE sign describes how you approach life's necessary changes.

PISCES: Its house shows where you need to cultivate and live on faith, while the . . .

12TH HOUSE sign describes the nature of your commitment to the future and the type of service that you can offer.

The Planets in Brief

The horoscope can be viewed as acts of a play unfolding. The HOUSES represent the stage. The SIGNS describe the setting and the PLANETS represent the actors. So far we have discovered that houses represent environmental experiences. Signs describe needs regarding these areas of life. Based on these needs, distinct personality traits emerge. These can be positive or negative depending on your degree of development, as you will discover in later chapters. Planets represent personality functions, or energies, which seek out, initiate or attract activities or circumstances which feed your needs, help you to develop your potentials and to build confidence.

Each sign is ruled by a specific planet, as the energy represented by the planet has the potential to fulfill the needs described by one or more signs. For example, Mars rules Aries. Aries describes the NEED for independence. Mars, as shown outlined below, represents the urge for action and therefore enables you to fulfill the pioneering instincts described by Aries.

The functions of the planets will be covered in greater depth later in the book. For now, the following keyword descriptions should suffice.

SUN .... Will, purpose, consciousness
MOON .... Emotions, responses, habits
MERCURY .... Mental process, logic
VENUS .... Power to attract, appreciation
MARS .... Action, desire
JUPITER .... Expansion, opportunity
SATURN .... Structure, discipline
URANUS .... Originality, rebellion
NEPTUNE .... Inspiration, idealism
PLUTO .... Power, regeneration

The Journey

Now let's begin our expedition through the signs to see more fully their significance in a horoscope's interpretation. As you read through the descriptions of each sign, remember that all twelve signs will be found somewhere within the structure of your chart! So, with chart in hand, begin by asking yourself . . .

"Who Am I?"

ARIES

While you may not find your "destiny" within the experiences ruled by the house of Aries, you WILL find a sense of direction here. Aries describes the need to know, within yourself, that you exist, you are capable of functioning independently and need not lean on others for support. Here is the sign of the pioneer, and while the trailblazing instincts may have been suppressed by some, they still lie dormant within, awaiting release, freedom and adventure. Aries encourages new experiences. With each new activity initiated in its house, a new adjective can be added to your self description. The keyphrase for Aries is "I AM." "I AM an individual. I AM daring. I AM strong. I AM." BUT . . . "I must PROVE this to myself by daring to move into new experiences yet unexplored, with no guarantee of success."

How many times have you heard someone say: "You'll never know until you try."? Or, "Doing something and making a mistake is better than never having tried at all." Both of these cliches are especially applicable to the sign, Aries. To venture into areas not yet explored requires courage. Yet, to remain fixed in one place, shutting the door to progress, is a crime against your soul. So here, in the area of life (house) ruled by Aries, the unknown calls. The challenge is not just to hear the call, but to ACT on it.

Seldom is there much objectivity concerning the matters of the Aries house. Here, instincts lead the way. Lessons come through experience. Being the first sign of the zodiac, Aries represents the first step leading to selfhood. The cardinal/energy, combined with the fire/enthusiasm, gives Aries a tremendous zest for life. The challenge of this sign is not to worry about the results, but to take the initiative to get things started. For some, the challenges are viewed as exciting, stimulating and desirable. Others find these same challenges particularly threatening, especially those with strong security urges, as any new activity requires moving beyond comfortable boundaries.

Even though it is important for you to realize your oneness with all others, this is not the role of Aries. You must first find a sense of personal identity before that identity can relate to others. So here, in Aries, you must prove to yourself, and to others, that you are a separate individual, just as a small child proves to himself that he is capable of taking his first step and in doing so PROVES that he has a free will. The Aries house describes where you need to prove this same concept. In doing so you will discover not only who you are today, but what you are capable of becoming tomorrow.

It is important to realize that no sign is better than any other. All twelve signs can be found in every chart. The challenge is one of integration. At the same time, all signs have the potential for both positive and negative expression. For example, you could, in the Aries ruled house, express a me-first attitude rather than considering how others might be affected by your actions. There is a tendency to develop a combative, sometimes destructive, temperament. While this does not imply that you will demonstrate the negative characteristics of the sign, it becomes a possibility. Being overly defensive concerning your need for independence, or feeling threatened by the outer demands made upon you, can lead to combative behavior or extreme self-involvement regarding the matters described by the house it rules in your chart.

The RAM has been chosen to symbolize Aries. We can imagine his head down with horns out front to fight if need be for what he desires. A ram does not move around obstacles which block his path. He meets issues head on, sometimes without the common sense to wait for better conditions or to recognize that it might be easier, and safer, to walk around barriers rather than trying to "butt" his way through them. These traits are not foreign to the Aries personality as Aries does not, at first, operate with much consciousness. Consciousness is a result of action. As you move further through your journey into the signs you will find how to control, or leash, the overly rash aspects of Aries without losing the spirit it represents.

The glyphs chosen to represent the signs were not chosen at random. They hold symbolic meaning which can help you to comprehend more deeply the significance of the signs they represent. The glyph of Aries (♈) can be viewed as the fountain of life, spilling forth life's vital energies. Others see it in the birth of spring, sprouts bursting forth from the earth to take their first breath. It can also be viewed as the horns of a ram, illustrating the strong will of the masculine force Aries represents.

It should be obvious at this point that everything starts at a psychological level in Aries via the energy provided by its ruling planet, Mars. New ideas are put into action. This action carries the potential to ripen into fruitful substances later in the cycle of the signs. The purpose of Aries does not include getting results. It does involve getting things started—activating, doing, living, and based on your daring, discovering your individual potentials through the independent activities you excite. Each day, for example, you have the opportunity to say "I AM" and add a new adjective to the previous day's description. Self awareness stems from unconscious potential which expresses itself, or comes to life, as a result of instinctive impulse. Each day you can discover something new about yourself. Aries is, indeed, the sign of CREATION. It is interesting that Easter is celebrated each year when the sun is moving through Aries, symbolizing the new life emerging from a physical form that the past no longer dominated.

Signs are also given rulership over specific parts of the physical anatomy and bodily functions. In the illustration of anatomical rulerships, you will find Aries rules the head.

Anatomical Rulerships

Aries . . . . Head as a whole
Taurus . . . . Neck & throat
Gemini . . . . Arms, hands, shoulders, lungs
Cancer . . . . Stomach & breasts
Leo . . . . Heart & back
Virgo . . . . Intestines
Libra . . . . Kidneys
Scorpio . . . . Eliminative & sexual organs
Sagittarius . . . . Hips & thighs
Capricorn . . . . Knees & bones
Aquarius . . . . Ankles & calves
Pisces . . . . Feet

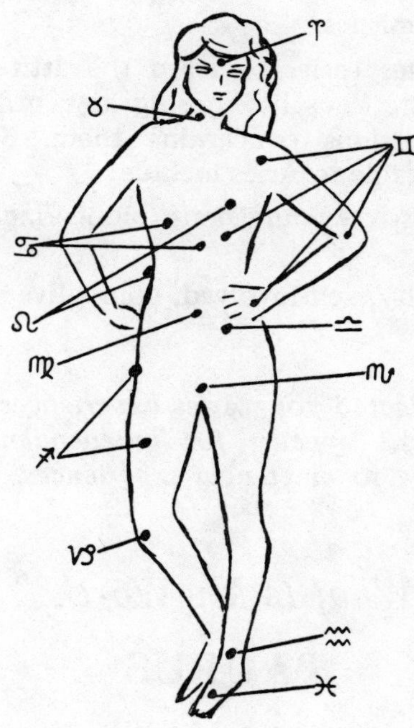

Research has revealed that people suffering from frequent headaches often complain (or maybe should be more aggressive in doing so) of being dominated by others, feeling that their Aries-independence and natural leadership skills are being threatened. The activities ruled by the house of Aries show what, or who, could be provoking those headaches. You may feel surrounded here, restricted by your environment or fearful of being self assertive and free. Head wounds are also Aries-ruled. Rather than representing repressed aggression or anger, facial and head wounds suggest excessive use of aggression. Acne is another Aries-ruled disease, especially prevalent in our youth and certainly demonstrating the identity-confusion experienced at this age. Anger and aggression, rather than, or along with, revealing itself through behavior problems, often erupt in facial blemishes.

It is sometimes easier to learn the attitudes and needs represented by the signs by chosing keywords which arouse images or impressions concerning them. Some keywords particularly applicable to Aries include:

POSITIVE: aggressive, courageous, pioneering, initiating, daring, instinctive.

NEGATIVE: pushy, self-involved, combative, defensive, careless, abrasive.

Having investigated your Aries experiences and discovered your separateness, capacity for independence and having developed courage to meet new experiences, you might next ask . . .

"What Is My Worth?"

TAURUS

Unlike Aries, Taurus is concerned with getting RESULTS for action. Therefore, Taurus is acutely aware of the degree of energy required to accomplish any given task. By observing the house of Taurus in your chart, you will find where you are being challenged to be productive, practical, to function with both feet planted firmly on the ground. Being a fixed/earth sign, it describes the need to be resourceful at a practical level.

Here, no longer concerned with action for action's sake only, you need to focus on the potential value or worth of all action. Through your Taurus experiences you learn to appreciate the tangible aspects and sensual enjoyments life has to offer. You need substance here and should be concerned with quality rather than quantity. Being an earth sign, Taurus has been associated with farming—getting down to basics, relating to the substances of the earth and appreciating its natural beauty as well as the physical pleasures available on our planet in our human form.

The keyphrase for Taurus is "I HAVE." "I HAVE strength. I HAVE power of perseverance. I HAVE substance. I HAVE form. I HAVE physical grace." The words, "I have," signify the need to get results from the new experiences initiated in the previous sign, Aries. "I HAVE something valuable and can prove its value by showing solid, substantial evidence." What is valuable to you here are those things having form, or that which can be appreciated and experienced via the five senses.

The Taurus keyphrase implies that there is substantial proof—physical evidence—that something exists or at least has the potential to exist in a physical sense. The goal connected with this area of your life (house) is to formulate and materialize things which demonstrate your values. Due to this need for "ownership" there is a tendency to become overly possessive of the substances acquired through your Taurus experiences. Changes become threatening here. Your roots at some time will need to be transplanted or you will become overly attached to the earth.

Change, however, is no easy task for Taurus. Therefore, in its house, you need practical, tangible proof of the validity or necessity of changing existing structures before taking action. Taurus has a "prove it to me" attitude toward new experiences and ideas. "Prove why I should change, or show me a practical reason for doing so, and only then will I even consider the possibility of doing so." This might characterize your approach to making adjustments in the Taurus department of your life. Yes, stubbornness can be one of the negative traits of Taurus. On the other hand, laziness is not foreign to the sign. As Taurus is acutely aware of the ingredients necessary to give an idea form, you must see some value in it before you are willing to exert your energy.

Its glyph (♉), from one point of view, is seen as the head of a bull, demonstrating the strength of this sign. From another level, the glyph, consisting of a combination of a circle (representing spirit) and the crescent moon (representing the mind) symbolizes the incarnation of spirit. The BULL is its symbol, or the picture chosen to represent Taurus, exemplifying the strength and determination of this sign; along with the stubborn streak it demonstrates. On the other hand, Ferdinand the Bull, shows the lazy side of Taurus as he sits under a tree, sniffing a daisy, enjoying the pleasures of the senses.

Taurus complements Aries, just as all feminine signs complement the preceding masculine force. Taurus consolidates the inspiration and progressive drive of Aries, giving it form and stability. What is started through the Aries ruled house must take root in Taurus if the cycle of the signs is to continue creatively.

Taurus finds security by possessing. This can develop into a materialistic outlook toward the matters of its house, or a tendency to accumulate substances without discrimination. At some point you must learn to let go, to weed out, in order to preserve order in your life. A little later on in our journey through the signs you will find where lessons of giving and releasing are learned. Here, in Taurus, the basic consideration is one of accumulation. As illustrated on page 37, Taurus rules the neck and throat. At one level, this provides Taurus with vocal talent. However, it is important to consider that it is via the throat that we take in food which sustains the body, and strengthens the mind. Taurus warns us not to over-indulge.

Possessiveness or greed, at one level, or lack of productivity and self worth at another, can lead to sore throats, thyroid problems and more. Tonsilitis in the young, for example, often corresponds to a period in a child's development when his or her worth is strongly challenged or in doubt. When sore throats interrupt your usually productive schedule, it might be wise to ask yourself, regarding the Taurus-ruled activities in your life: What is it that you can't swallow? Who is challenging your values? To what material or physical pleasures have you become overly attached? Or, just what are you taking for granted?

Some keywords applicable to Taurus include:

POSITIVE: determined, resourceful, persevering, practical, sense-aware.

NEGATIVE: stubborn, miserly, bull-headed, lazy, self-indulgent.

Once basic requirements for survival are secured through the Aries and Taurus activities, the intellect has time to unfold. Therefore, from here you might ask . . .

"How Can I Learn?"

GEMINI

In Gemini, curiosity is developed which opens the door to learning, versatility and CHOICE. Of all areas in your chart, the experiences ruled by Gemini's house require the greatest flexibility. Gemini thrives on change, because variety offers food for thought, which develops objective thinking patterns. Here, in the house of Gemini, curiosity is aroused which motivates you to seek out new experiences having educational value. You need communication here, because contacts made with others and exposure to the knowledge available in your surroundings are the only means by which your many questions can be answered.

Due to the variety of experiences you initiate and those required of you within the area of life ruled by Gemini, certain contradictions in your own personality emerge. These contradictions stem from the opposite concepts brought out through your Aries and Taurus experiences. Aries is aggressive; Taurus is passive. As both qualities are now evident in your personality, integration becomes necessary. The duality of Gemini ultimately cultivates objectivity, the ability to see things from more than one point of view. Contacts made with others in your environment stir up new ideas which challenge you to see views foreign from your own. The possessive tendency of Taurus and the inherent self involvement of Aries are modified.

The keyphrase for Gemini is "I THINK." "I THINK about the choices available to me. I THINK about what I have seen and heard." While Gemini shows where thinking primarily dominates, this sign, in itself, is not concerned with the physical manifestation of ideas. Here, you accumulate information enabling you later to dissect, perfect and make adjustments accordingly. For this reason, people who get "stuck" in the Gemini experience often seem shallow or superficial, skimming over the surface of multiple topics without ever getting to the point or the depth of the matter. As the cycle of the signs continues to unfold, greater objectivity and a deeper perspective is developed.

It is rare to find only one issue involved with the experiences ruled by Gemini's house. The duality of the sign attracts variety. For example, those having Gemini on the 2nd house, ruling finances, often have two different sources of income. Those with Gemini on the 5th, ruling offspring, more often than not have only two children. Gemini is referred to as a "Jack of all trades, master of none." This saying may strike home as you assess the area of life ruled by the house it occupies in your own chart. There is a tendency to collect a little bit of information about a large number of subjects, as Gemini's purpose is to arouse curiosity about what lies ahead.

The twins, Castor and Pollux, have been chosen to symbolize Gemini, demonstrating the total concept of duality and choice—good/bad, right/left, male/female, right/wrong, even to include the right and left functioning of the brain, or the conscious and unconscious mind. It is interesting to note that many people with strong Gemini traits are ambidextrous, another example of Gemini's capacity for adaptability. This sign has the ability to link opposite forces, as exemplified by its glyph (♊). The glyph represents the options open to Gemini. Here, we find the Pillars of Hercules. The pillars are joined, representing the ability to use the intellect to link the self to substance.

One of Gemini's greatest talents involves communication. Words enable you to connect and make associations with what is going on between yourself and others. People having Gemini strongly emphasized in their charts seem to have the right word for any occasion. From a positive point of view, this provides literary talent and communication skills. Used negatively, however, Gemini uses words to avoid facing issues of real importance. Verbal deception is not totally foreign to this sign, nor is verbal manipulation. If you wish, you could make no conscious effort to integrate the various experiences accumulated through the activities available in your Gemini house, but instead, enjoy the two different lives you live, keeping everyone guessing who you are today versus who you will be tomorrow.

Here, in Gemini, there is a need for adventure, if only in the realm of the mind. The mind is active, quickly moving from one thought to another, gaining new ideas through each mental expedition. Due to the variety of interests involved here, it isn't any wonder that Gemini rules a variety of maladies and bodily functions. As shown in the illustration on page 37, Gemini rules the arms, hands, shoulders, lungs and basic nervous system.

When you have spread yourself too thin in the area of life ruled by Gemini's house, nervous conditions are sure to result. When you have your fingers in too many pies, one of them is bound to get injured. Look at the hands of a Gemini and notice how often you find scars there. These are little reminders of past errors in judgement. Excess smoking, excessive hand gestures or arm thrashing are other symptoms of taxed nerves.

Tension often settles in the shoulders. This is your body's way of telling you that it is time to relax. Instead of using your lungs for communicating superficial gibberish, or abusing them with smoke, try a few deep breathing exercises when your Gemini experiences get out of hand. In channeling the mental energy available here you will find these diseases rapidly disappearing. In general, it is safe to say that medical problems or injuries involving these bodily functions stem from excessive mental activity OR the repression of your intellectual curiosity and learning potential.

The mutable/versatility, air/intellectuality and masculine/assertiveness, when combined, certainly give a clear outline of the Gemini message. Some keywords to help you remember the Gemini needs include:

POSITIVE: communicative, interesting, flexible, witty, intelligent, curious.

NEGATIVE: scattered, superficial, unreliable, changeable, gossipy, manipulative.

Once having mingled with the environment, communicated with others, gained new ideas from your experiences and discovered your capacity to reason, you'll soon recognize the need to build boundaries around experiences which provide security. This awareness leads you to ask . . .

"Where Do I Belong?"

CANCER

The house ruled by Cancer shows where, moved by emotion, you seek out experiences which secure your Aries-identity and build foundations in your personal life. At first insecurity is experienced toward the matters ruled by Cancer's house. Here, the need to belong becomes a major concern. The challenge of Cancer is to develop security by nurturing experiences rather than clinging to, or depending on, the strengths of others. Once personal security is acquired, Cancer no longer "feeds" on the strengths of the environment, but begins to nurture those very things that once it fed upon. On the other hand, no other sign finds such ease in nurturing the habits of the past and developing dependencies on them than the insecure Cancer.

Cancer is the most family-oriented of all twelve signs, and is frequently described as the sign of motherhood. The approach taken to the matters of Cancer's house can be likened to the approach a mother might take toward protecting and nurturing her young. Here, you need warmth, nurturing and love and will attack if, and when, security boundaries are threatened.

At first your Cancer instincts are expressed at a very personal level, such as in self protection, maintaining family unity and concern for protective barriers. As confidence is developed, the security boundaries begin to expand until you reach out beyond the immediate and apply your nurturing talent toward accomplishing social goals. Then, you become the "counselor," helping others find the security and belongingness you once fought so hard to achieve.

Within the experiences of Cancer's house you function not on the basis of logic, but according to "gut feeling." Your approach to these activities must be a cautious one in order to avoid upsetting the status quo. While Cancer is a cardinal/assertive sign, it is of the water/emotional element and in the feminine/passive gender. This combination tells us that Cancer will take action and can be assertive, but does so cautiously and according to feeling. The tendency to attach yourself to the comfortable patterns of the past manifests in the cautious approach you take toward changes in this area of your life. Yes, being a cardinal sign, you will act here; you will fight. But, only when an issue attacks the very core of your security and walking around issues no longer works.

The keyphrase for Cancer is "I FEEL." "I FEEL secure. I FEEL contented. I FEEL at home with myself." BUT . . . to feel truly secure here, you must first be willing to let go of the past and adapt to the changing times. This is one of the greatest challenges confronted in the Cancer area of your life. At first you tend NOT to feel independent (Cancer on 1st house), self sufficient (Cancer on 2nd house), informed (Cancer on 3rd house), etc., but must develop this outlook through experience.

In Cancer you learn to define boundaries, live within them and to understand the significance of them before progress can be viewed as non-threatening. This sign, along with its ruler, the Moon, rules the memory where remnants of all past experiences are stored. For this reason, when involved with the experiences of its house, it is easy to live in a world of memory, in the past, with no desire to move toward tomorrow.

Your emotional responses and stability are shaped by early life involvements. Based on these experiences, certain reactions develop. In otherwords, you would not have a particular response to any life situation had some experience from the past not pre-shaped it. In Cancer's house you have ties with that past. Memories from yesterday to the beginning of life are stored here. The need is not to identify with them, but to use the knowledge gained from the past as a foundation for the future.

The crab has been chosen to symbolize Cancer, as its physical and behavioral characteristics exemplify the personality traits of this sign. The crab, for example, walks sideways, avoiding direct confrontation with obstacles. So describes the Cancer individual. The crab has a hard outer shell which protects its inner softness. You, too, tend to build a shell around your inner sensitivity and vulnerability regarding the area of life ruled by Cancer's house. A crab will hold on to its prey long after its own life has been threatened. In the Cancer house of your chart, you tend to hang on to security, or loved ones, sometimes too tightly, until those very things, or people, you want to protect have suffocated.

The glyph of Cancer (♋) can be seen as the claws of a crab, or more appropriately, the female uterus which protects and nurtures that which has not yet reached maturity. Others associate the glyph with the female breasts. When family pressures or feelings of sterility involving this area of your life get out of hand, the breasts and/or stomach could feel the effect. Research has shown that women developing breast tumors or cysts have had recent problems with family or changes in the home which "uproot" them emotionally in some way.

Ulcers are definitely a result of emotional stress. Next time your stomach starts acting up, ask yourself: What's going on in your life that you can't quite stomach? Rather than nurturing the problems surrounding you and watching them grow, try releasing your hold with love.

Some keywords appropriate to the Cancer needs and attitudes include:

POSITIVE: nurturing, warm, protective, sensitive, receptive.

NEGATIVE: clinging, moody, clannish, non-progressive, fearful.

Once having established boundaries which protect and promise security, your next challenge involves finding creative outlets which help you to maintain your emotional equilibrium. So, from here, the next question regarding self development might be . . .

"What Is My Importance?"

LEO

In Leo you need to see yourself reflected through creative modes of expression and in others' responses to you until self consciousness and a sense of personal importance are cultivated. When involved with the experiences described by

Leo's house you need to be the center of attention. You need to feel confident that you are in charge of this department of your life, that you stand out, you are charismatic, you have the capacity to leave your personal insignia on all that you touch and on all those who touch you. Doing so acts as a reminder to yourself and to others that you not only exist (Aries) but you are important.

A strong, sometimes unbending, will accompanies your approach to the matters ruled by Leo's house. The primary need here is to understand the importance of your individual role in the unfoldment of the experiences ruled by the house involved. To become conscious of, and to continually re-affirm, your importance requires constant reassurance from others. For this reason you need more attention in your Leo house than elsewhere in your life.

If, up until this point, the cycle of the signs (from Aries through Cancer) has unfolded creatively, the Leo house shows where benefits are found and self-confidence is expressed at a highly creative level. Special attention will naturally and automatically be given. On the other hand, if you have failed to cultivate the positive qualities of the first four signs you will project your insecurities in one of two ways:

1. a tendency to demand undeserved attention which gives you an artificial sense of importance, or . . .

2. an inability to accept recognition and praise when offered which, in itself, is an attention-getting technique.

The point to be stressed here is Leo's need to feel purposeful, the need for recognition and the need to take pride in personal accomplishments without getting caught up in the glory of that self esteem.

The keyphrase given to Leo is "I WILL." Don't mistake this for a statement of passivity, but rather one of strength and commitment. "I WILL this to be. My WILL be done." The ego development of Leo is powerful. It can be used to overpower others in an attempt to prove your importance or it can be directed toward achieving a purposeful goal. As shown by the brief, but powerful keyphrase, Leo shows where you have the power to create, to make things happen by using your will. Being a fixed/determined, fire/goal-oriented sign, Leo contains all the ingredients for success.

The expressive talent of Leo makes it the most dramatic of all twelve signs. There is a tendency, in fact, to build things out of proportion when confronting the matters ruled by its house or to over-react to conditions as they unfold. Here, you put your whole heart into what you are doing. At the same time, you are big hearted when others are in need. The generosity so often associated with Leo not only benefits those who gain from your giving, but feeds your own ego. It is wise to occasionally stop and examine the Leo area of your life in reference to your underlying motives regarding your generosity. Ask yourself: Do you give because you truly enjoy giving pleasure to others? OR, are you unconsciously looking for the praise and approval that comes as a result? Are you, in fact, feeding your own ego with your offerings, knowing the responses that your generosity brings?

The symbol chosen to represent Leo is the LION. The lion personifies the power to reign over the experiences, or the "kingdom" described by its house placement in the chart. If insecure, Leo is seen in the archetype of the cowardly lion, wanting to be strong, needing to be appreciated, but feeling inadequate due to insecurities carried over from the past (Cancer). In its glyph (♌) you will find the lion's tail or, from another point of view, the seed of life (sperm), referring to Leo's concern for survival of the spirit through reproduction and creativity.

As shown in the illustration on page 37, Leo rules the heart and spine. If these are weak zones in your body, you might ask yourself the following questions: If your back pains you, have you taken on too great a load in the area of life described by your Leo house because you're too proud to ask for help? Can you "bend" your will without feeling spineless?

Heart patients often confess to a growing fear of not being appreciated. Some have literally suffered from a broken heart. Senior citizens could feel unloved and unproductive to the extent that their egos are destroyed as is the most vital organ of the body, the heart. One might ask: Is heart failure really due to old age or is it a symptom of the loss of one's life purpose?

Some keywords which can help you more easily to recall the Leo message include:

POSITIVE: creative, generous, purposeful, dramatic, expressive, powerful.

NEGATIVE: egotistical, willful, conceited, overly theatrical, demanding.

Soon the identity born in Aries will be ready to meet others on a one-to-one basis. But first, one more step must be taken, one more question confronted . . .

"Can I Adapt?"

VIRGO

The next step taken on your journey through the signs reveals a detour requiring unforeseen adjustments. The experiences offered in Virgo's house require you to slow down in order to assess just how far you have come and to determine what adjustments are needed if further progress is to be made. The experiences gathered through Virgo's house require a critical assessment and reorientation. Here, you must ask yourself: What facets of my personality need improvement? Where, up until now, have I over extended myself?

Were you overly aggressive in your Aries activities? Perhaps you have become overly attached to your Taurus-ruled senses. Did you scatter yourself in Gemini? Have you learned, through your Cancer involvements, to define personal boundaries and handle your emotions? Have you become trapped by your own Leo pride? Has your need for attention gotten out of hand? If so, the experiences attracted in Virgo's house will make you aware of what needs YOUR attention.

The activities provided by Virgo call for detailed analysis and perfection of techniques. Here, acutely aware of imperfection, you take things apart, piece by piece, trying to find better techniques for functioning than those originally practiced. It is said that Virgo can't see the forest for the trees. While this might be true, it is the primary goal of this sign to see and to appreciate the details that go into any creation or idea.

In the house of Virgo you need to analyze, perfect and digest all that has been absorbed through previous experiences in an attempt to find a useful application for acquired skills. The goal is not to become trapped in the detail, but to develop an appreciation for it. The experiences offered here require analysis, assessment, digestion and the elimination of those things that have proven unfit for future use. This process not only involves mental discrimination, but physical processes as well. Routines must be developed, schedules must be made and kept, if there is to be organization in this department of your life.

Due to the analytical faculties developed through your Virgo experiences, you find where and what adjustments must be made in your personal life in order to assure successful relationships later in the cycle of the signs. Here, in Virgo, you are encouraged to organize your personal life, work at perfecting flaws and develop more objectivity concerning life and its meaning. Its house shows where a psychological house cleaning is in order.

It is easy, in the process of your self critique, to get caught up in your imperfections to the degree that you lose sight of your overall potential. This develops into unrealistic worries over insignificant details, hypochondria in regard to health or an overly critical outlook on life in general. For this reason, it is important, regarding your Virgo ruled house, to avoid turning your productive, analytical talents into a critical or calculating projection.

The keyphrase for Virgo is "I ANALYZE." Virgo's talent for zoning in on imperfections and developing techniques by which to make improvements makes this sign especially useful when situations have gotten out of hand and organization is needed. A degree of humility is developed through the experiences of this house as you learn to fulfill useful, routine, necessary tasks even though they may not bring personal recognition.

The Virgin symbolizes the attempt to reach a state of perfection in the area of life ruled by Virgo. For Virgo's symbol you will find a maiden carrying a sheaf of wheat, signifying both purity (virgin) and the dedication required for a successful harvest. Virgo's glyph (♍) was taken from the first letter of the Greek word for virgin. It is an ideograph of the female generative organs, with the hook representing the virgin state.

As it is the purpose of Virgo to distinguish the difference between what is valuable and useful and what is superficial waste material, it does not seem surprising that it has been given physiological rulership over the intestines. Just as information and experiences are absorbed and analyzed to find the value contained within, so the body must discriminate the value of what has been ingested. Food is processed in the intestines. Part of its substance is absorbed into the body through the intestinal walls, while some is prepared for elimination. Failure to use discrimination concerning what is "fed" into the Virgo experiences of your life could easily cause intestinal discomfort.

If you suffer from such disease, ask yourself, concerning your Virgo ruled activities: Are you responsible and organized in your daily life? Are you fulfilling a useful role here? Are you being discriminating in service—willing, while still enabling others to help themselves?

Some keywords to help you remember the main message of Virgo include:

POSITIVE: discriminating, useful, efficient, organized, detailed, analytical.

NEGATIVE: critical, complaining, perfectionistic, puritanical, worrisome.

You're Halfway Home

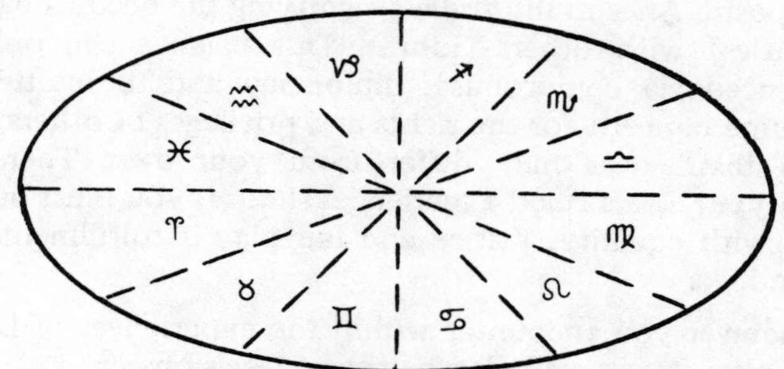

You have now traveled to the midpoint of your journey through the zodiac. The avenues of development thus far experienced have involved personal growth only. From this point on you will no longer travel alone, as all future activities will involve others. A whole new vista of experience is soon to be seen . . .

"Can I Relate?"

LIBRA

All lessons of Libra involve the realization and integration of opposites, particularly those contrasts found within personal relationships. The primary purpose of this sign is one of sharing—sharing ideas, sharing experiences, sharing your life—with others. Here, in Libra's house you need to develop a healthy balance between personal goals and respect for the goals of others. This, in itself, is no easy task. As you exchange ideas and experiences with others, objectivity is developed—the ability to see things from another's point of view. Libra shows where you need relationships which offer feedback which, in turn, help you develop into a more objective, "other-oriented" individual.

As shown in the illustration on the previous page, Libra lies opposite Aries in the zodiac, signifying the need to balance self (Aries) with others (Libra). This balance can only be experienced via compromise, diplomacy and the cultivation of genuine concern for the rights and privileges of others, even though their ideas may differ from your own. Therefore, toward your Libra ruled experiences (house) you must be concerned with equality, justice and fair play if fulfillment is to be found.

Whatever you encounter within the experiences of Libra's house, alternatives will also be there. Decisions are not easily made as you can see the value, and the flaws, in all choices offered. Thus, the capacity for compromise without total sacrifice and the integration of opposites is needed. The challenge is to find ways of integrating seemingly opposite points of view. Libra then becomes the moderator, the go-between and often, due to this very talent, shows where you find it difficult to make firm decisions when alternatives present themselves. The choices of Libra, unlike those of Gemini, involve finding ways of integrating two seemingly different units, while Gemini is making a choice to follow one of two paths.

Much will be learned by watching and listening to others' feedback to your approach to the matters ruled by Libra's house. You find yourself "mirrored" through the actions of others when functioning here. If you fail to consider their needs, a sense of isolation and sometimes defensiveness becomes apparent. Where, in your life, is the universe encouraging you to share? Where is your happiness dependent on your ability to compromise? The keyphrase for Libra is "I BALANCE" or "I SHARE," signifying the need to create harmony by sharing cooperatively with others.

From a positive point of view, the challenges of Libra lead to the capacity to share without fear that your own identity (Aries) has been threatened in any way. Sharing, after all, implies two or more people working cooperatively with one another with no one person taking the full load or the total credit. To work with others on a one-to-one basis, without losing your capacity for independence, requires mutual cooperation between yourself and those around you.

Negatively, Libra can show where you attempt to manipulate others. You have a talent for appearing diplomatic and concerned while actually using your manipulative grace to get your own way. On the other hand, if Aries has not been developed, and you fear "doing your own thing" you could lean on others here, requesting and/or allowing others to make choices for you. The negative Libra tends to thrive on keeping people and conditions out of balance. If the first six signs were not developed positively you might create, or attract, issues that upset the status quo for no other reason than to sit back and enjoy the resulting disharmony.

The picture chosen to represent Libra is the SCALES OF JUSTICE, symbolizing both the need to keep life balanced and the sensitivity to imbalances so evident in this sign. Total and complete equality is necessary in your Libra house if your scales are to remain balanced. "Weighing" issues is important here. Its glyph (♎) represents the sun setting over the western horizon. Notice that the sun is half above and half below the horizon, half visible and half not. This represents the counterpart of each individual found through a partner or a mate.

Imbalances in the experiences ruled by Libra which are not met outwardly can also create an imbalance in the bodily functioning, especially through kidney disorders. As shown on page 37, Libra rules the kidneys. The role of the kidneys is to purify the body of toxins and irritants. When relationships become "poisonous" to the point that you lose yourself to another, kidney malfunctions are more likely to occur. In such cases, examine your Libra house to find where these imbalances or injustices are evident. A craving for a partner or a mate with whom to share your life, when left unfilled at an outer level, could result in a craving for "sweets" which subsequently encourages diabetes (another Libra ruled disease).

"No one ever promised life would be fair." It's up to each one of us to do what we can to make it so. Sharing, working side-by-side with others, seeing the needs of others as equally important as your own without losing your identity in the process, can help you put an end to physical, psychological, social and spiritual imbalances.

Some keywords to help you recall the essence of Libra include:

POSITIVE: cooperative, balanced, artistic, diplomatic, concerned.

NEGATIVE: manipulative, indecisive, easily-swayed by others, vain, superficial.

The relationships cultivated through the experiences of Libra's house soon reveal a new, previously unforeseen challenge. You become aware, through the feedback of others, of a need to eliminate past ego-centered involvements in order to maintain the relationships recently established. So, from here, a new question is formed . . .

"What Must I Change?"

SCORPIO

Scorpio's house shows where regeneration is needed. The goal here is to unite your energies and potentials with those of others so that, as a team, you can produce something more valuable than any of you, as individuals, could have produced separately. Therefore, the urge to maintain control over outer circumstances for personal gain only no longer has value.

Dependencies, resentments and superstitions built around past experiences, or a desire for power, must be confronted in Scorpio. In essence, the identity discovered in Aries must be reborn if life from here on is to bring further fulfillment and growth. The test of Scorpio is one of elimination, regeneration and sometimes sacrifice. Can you let go of your attachment to the past so that the present can exist and the future can unfold? The need to do so becomes evident through the experiences attracted in Scorpio's house. Here is where regeneration begins.

This does not imply that the fruits of past labors must be eliminated altogether, but acts as a reminder that an attachment to them does not induce further growth. The question is: Will you hold on to those things that once brought about growth and power at the expense of the new opportunities available further ahead on your journey through the signs? Where do you draw the line?

As shown on page 53, Scorpio lies opposite Taurus in the zodiac. Taurus accumulates; Scorpio eliminates. This polarity provides an awareness of attitudes and possessions that have outlived their usefulness and therefore must be eliminated if further progress is to be made. Taurus, on one hand, describes the need to accumulate self sustaining assets. At some point in your life, however, those assets will become obsolete or "spoiled." When this happens, Scorpio encourages you to weed out, clean house and throw out those things you have outgrown. On the other hand, without Taurus, Scorpio would have no substances to regenerate. If this polarity is not integrated there is a tendency to accumulate indiscriminately or to eliminate assets still having value.

Being a fixed/water sign, Scorpio provides emotional endurance. It deals with past memories which have been repressed or trapped in the subconscious. Fears, desires or feelings of inadequacy must be brought to the surface and recycled so new experiences and knowledge can fill their spaces. The keyphrase for Scorpio is "I DESIRE," expressing the need to control personal desire and to regenerate the selfish motives which inhibit group interaction and productivity. The keyphrase "I REGENERATE" might, however, be more applicable to the true purpose of this sign.

The changes experienced as a result of deep involvement and investigation into the experiences ruled by Scorpio's house lead to this ego regeneration. Here, your intensity and perceptivity contribute to your ultimate rebirth. There is a need to look under the surface of the experiences encountered in Scorpio's house to evaluate underlying motives concerning your previous approach to them. The intensity of your investigation becomes strong, as does the impact of the results of what you find. By looking deeply into the significance of the Scorpio experiences, you will be changed, reborn, and become a new person with a broader outlook on life. This probing process, however, is a sensitive one as some of the material you dredge up from the subconscious may cause some discomfort until the process of regeneration has been completed.

It is important, in your process of elimination, not to eliminate, or annihilate those things or people still having a significant purpose in your life. From a negative level, no other sign has the power to destroy itself or others quite as thoroughly as the misdirected Scorpion. As evident in the experiences encountered in its house, it is a sign of extremes. You find here the perception of an indepth psychiatrist as well as the destruction of the psychopath. For this reason Scorpio has been given two symbolic representatives—the SCORPION, showing the lesser evolved Scorpio traits as illustrated by the scorpion's fatal sting and the PHOENIX, symbolizing the opportunity for rebirth.

As you look at the glyph for Scorpio (♏), notice its similarity to that chosen for Virgo. The similarity is striking and often confusing. The glyph for Virgo has a hook going through the side (♍), while that of Scorpio has an arrow. Virgo's purity has been pierced at this point of the cycle, and life will no longer be the same. The unity and the sacrifices of relationships (and the death and rebirth that result from them) can be seen within this hieroglyphic.

As release or letting go is one of the major lessons of Scorpio, resentments that hang on, a fear of letting go of the past, the excessive drive to control, can easily lead to blockages in the body's elimination process. Constipation, hemorrhoids, as well as problems associated with the external sexual organs stem from insecurities in, or misdirected energies projected into, the Scorpio area of your life.

If these diseases are interfering with your creative development you might ask yourself: What resentments or fears are holding you back? What pains you to the degree that you no longer can sit down due to the pain this resentment has caused you? Wouldn't it be easier to release your hold with love? Scorpio's house gives a clue to where these problems originated.

Some keywords which will help you to recall the essence of the Scorpio experience include:
POSITIVE: intense, deep, controlled, powerful, perceptive, regenerating.
NEGATIVE: possessive, controlling, suspicious, vindictive, destructive.

After Scorpio completes its process of regeneration and elimination, new aspirations and opportunities for expansion become evident. Visions of future promises take form as you prepare to enter the world of Sagittarius where a new question is posed . . .

"How Far Can I Go?"

SAGITTARIUS

While in Scorpio you are required to investigate the depths of your own reality, Sagittarius offers experiences which encourage you to look ahead. Here, your needs are vast, your thirst for a social direction is intense and with this expanded outlook comes a new philosophy toward life and its meaning. In the house of Sagittarius the future beckons. You need to look ahead, broaden your horizons and seek out experiences which cultivate wisdom. Your concern here should no longer be centered around your relationship with those close to you, but needs to include a broader frame of reference. The knowledge sought here can only be found by looking beyond the immediate, expanding your horizons to include a more far-reaching territory.

It is said that experience breeds wisdom. This truth will be confirmed through the activities available in your Sagittarius house. Remaining open to new experiences cultivates ethical principles along with a philosophical and open minded outlook. An understanding of cultural differences at multi-levels is also important here. In essence, Sagittarius shows where you come to understand that you not only exist within the world, but that the world can exist within you. If not offered the opportunity to see the world through objective experience, dare to investigate "foreign" concepts by learning and through visualization. By doing so you will find that your opportunities to expand are limitless.

While water signs show where you tend to live in the past, the houses ruled by the fire signs (particularly Sagittarius) describe where you live for the future. Therefore, in this department of your life you need a goal to aim toward. You need to know that there is always something to look forward to, an opportunity for growth, expansion and promotion. When a current goal is met a new one must take its place or boredom soon sets in. For this reason a "don't fence me in" attitude may characterize your approach to these matters. Here, you need room to expand. You need room to breathe. You need space.

The keyphrase, "I UNDERSTAND," certainly describes the true essence of Sagittarius. Expansion and understanding stem from the experiences met within the area of life described by its house. Unlike Gemini, its polar opposite, Sagittarius is concerned with the *meaning* of experience rather than the experience itself. Words are assessed according to their philosophical value rather than from a purely literary point of view. You might say that what Gemini lacks, Sagittarius provides and vice versa. Gemini offers the words through which Sagittarius can express its abstractions. Sagittarius, on the other hand, gives wisdom to the words spoken by Gemini. As in the case of all opposing signs, integration is necessary.

Sagittarius is seen illustrated as a CENTAUR, half man/half horse. Here you find the body of a horse (strength) with the head of a man (intelligence) symbolizing the desire to let your mind roam freely. Its glyph (♐) is an arrow pointing upward, suggesting the power of Sagittarius to aim at lofty goals and to communicate ideas with such piercing conviction that all who come in touch with the abstractions are enlightened by them.

At a negative level, the need for freedom so prevalent in this sign can easily become a copout for not facing responsibility. Your need for space makes it difficult to cope with experiences which tie you down. At the same time, the need for openness and complete honesty in all things might reveal itself through blunt and sometimes hurtful communication. It is important to cultivate tact along with honesty and remember that while your sights must always be focussed on the promise of tomorrow you must still deal with the realities of today. The harder you try to avoid these realities the more likely you are to confront them.

As an example of how such confrontation might come about, consider the fact that Sagittarius rules the hips and upper legs. A broken leg or an arthritic hip will certainly bring you down to earth where escape is no longer a choice. Obesity, liver malfunctions and alcoholism are also Sagittarius related diseases. Overeating and/or drinking stem from an inability to draw limits, to see the potential of what lies ahead or from a total dissatisfaction with the realities at hand. Learning to live one day at a time might be helpful in dealing with problems involving excess. Focus is the keynote here. Yes, you need to see the potential of the future. You need to understand the larger, more philosophical point of view. Yet, you also need to bring these ideals down to a level where they can function creatively in your life to avoid such Sagittarius disorders.

Some keywords to help you remember the Sagittarius characteristics include:

POSITIVE: expansive, optimistic, visionary, honest, philosophical, open-minded.

NEGATIVE: excessive, fanatical, dishonest, blunt, irresponsible.

Having ventured into the world and seen its vastness, having met new experiences which have expanded your understanding, you are now ready to take another important step toward wholeness and enter the realm of Capricorn to confront a new challenge. Here, you must take a long, hard look at your life and ask . . .

"What Is My Social Role?"

CAPRICORN

The experiences met in Capricorn's house challenge you to define your individual role within society AND to accept the responsibilities that go along with that territory. The main issue in this department of your life (house) involves finding a responsible social place and establishing security within it. The challenge of Capricorn requires perseverance and hard work. While things may not come easily here, efforts will be rewarded if your energies are channeled constructively. In Capricorn you must earn the recognition and success you desire and must cultivate a willingness to accept the responsibilities that success entails, regardless of what your definition of success might be. Achievement is the keynote here.

Capricorn is not one of the easier signs of the zodiac. The responsibilities and limitations encountered in this area of your life can be burdensome as definite restrictions are placed on your activities. The challenge is to USE, constructively, those things available within the limits surrounding you before the boundaries will be extended. At the same time, the sense of accomplishment stemming from disciplined activity and concentrated energy can be extremely fulfilling when what you have been working toward, what you have earned through hard work, begins to materialize.

In essence, Capricorn creates the need to define, and then to find, your "space," to know where you belong and to understand the importance of your social role, no matter how great or small that role might seem. You will undoubtedly be challenged in Capricorn's house to conform, to be conservative, to be responsible and law-abiding. Later in the cycle of the signs you will have more freedom to be unconventional. For now, in Capricorn, you must learn to live with structure, acknowledging your place in society and playing your part in maintaining its stability. By realizing and accepting the fact that you ARE a part of the larger structure you become more aware of your obligation to contribute to it.

Self-doubt, lack of confidence and pessimism could, at first, characterize your approach to your Capricorn activities. It is only after you have proven yourself socially, through tangible accomplishments, that you will find security in this area of your life. As illustrated on page 53, Capricorn lies opposite Cancer in the zodiac. It was the role of Cancer to establish security at a personal, emotional level through family and other close contacts. Capricorn provides an opportunity to establish a sense of "social security." As with all opposites, what one sign lacks, the opposite provides. In this polarity, Capricorn finds warmth through Cancer while giving it some structure and protection from emotional wounds. Without the polarity of Cancer, you could easily become obsessed with what others think, ignoring what others might need. Human warmth could be replaced by an extreme ambition to achieve social status.

The keyphrase for Capricorn, "I USE," can be interpreted in two distinctly different ways. Positively, Capricorn encourages you to USE what is available to you with little or no waste. Negatively, however, there is a tendency to "use" others for one's own advantage. Personal prestige should not stem from another's failure. So, in Capricorn, you need to know your social place as separate from others and be ready to defend your territory, but also be careful not to trespass on the territory rightfully belonging to another.

The picture chosen to portray Capricorn is the mountain goat. The goat exemplifies the determination, ambition and drive of this sign. He is willing to climb from the bottom to the top, over rocky terrain if necessary, to achieve his mission. There are few things more awesome than a picture of the rugged mountain goat standing atop the territory he has claimed for his own. Although not easily recognized, its glyph consists of the head of a goat and the tail of a fish (♑), symbolizing the potential to rise from the depths (ocean) to the heights of human experience through determination and hard work.

In the house of Capricorn you need respect. Here, the challenge is to define your territory and attain success. Capricorn experiences demand from you that you abide by the laws set within the structure of your community. Yet, in the process of conforming it is easy to get caught up with the structures, expectations, regulations and limitations of society to the degree that you lose your individuality and flexibility both psychologically and physically.

Capricorn rules the skeletal frame and particularly the knees—the body's ability to "bend." If your bones become brittle, could it be because attitudes have become so crystallized that a minor "quake" would shatter them? Have you identified so strongly with your ambitions and ideas that you can no longer adapt to the new experiences life has to offer? Are your attitudes so rigid that you can't bend your knees in humble prayer? Humility is the test here. Can you find security within the structure of your life without becoming authoritative or judgemental concerning the role of others around you?

Some keywords to help you remember the characteristics of Capricorn include:

POSITIVE: responsible, successful, ambitious, hard working, respectful.

NEGATIVE: judgemental, authoritative, rigid, pessimistic, a user.

Only after having viewed the total picture can you objectively criticize the painting, or for that matter, the artist's vision. Likewise, only after becoming a part of the larger social experience, having learned of and lived by the laws of the community, can you objectively see the flaws in that system. In Capricorn you play your part in the social structure and as a result, discover what role you can play in changing what has proven undesirable or obsolete. When you have reached this level you are ready to enter the world of Aquarius to ask . . .

"What More Can I Do?"

AQUARIUS

While Capricorn provides structure in which to define your social role in practical terms, if the zodiac were to end here society would never progress, nor would you have an opportunity to grow beyond the "norm." Aquarius shows where you need to take one step beyond the predetermined path and break out of rigid conditioning to discover that you are more than what you were taught to be. You are, in truth, a unique individual.

In Aquarius you discover new adventures that challenge you to develop intellectually beyond controlled learning. In its house you are encouraged NOT to conform, but to REFORM and if necessary to rebel against social conditions or systems that have become obsolete. The keynote of Aquarius is progress. Ingenuity, inventiveness and the expression of originality are important here.

No longer limited by conventional boundaries, you are free to be different, to be inventive, to be yourself. You have learned independence from instinctive behavior (Aries); you have learned to appreciate the tangible gifts of life (Taurus); you have become educated through the environment and communicated with those in it (Gemini); you have experienced a sense of belongingness in a human sense (Cancer); you have seen your own importance and discovered a sense of purpose to your life (Leo); you have learned to discriminate and to use information wisely (Virgo); you have learned cooperation with others (Libra) and have experienced the regeneration that relationships induce (Scorpio); you have expanded your activities and thoughts to include a larger society (Sagittarius) and have established your territory within it (Capricorn). Now, in Aquarius, you are free to experiment with the knowledge you have gained to see if you can find new techniques to assist in society's future development—to break through society's fences.

To be truly creative, truly unique or to contribute your utmost to humanitarian progress, you must dare to break away from established social customs, to go one step further and investigate the potentials of tomorrow. If you cannot break from conventional ideas which hinder the expression of your intuitive wisdom you will become crystallized in your Capricorn experience until you are unable to move forward to accept, or take part in, our ever-changing world. You become stuck in a rut you have built for yourself or one you have allowed society to build for you.

Ideally, the progressive vision of Aquarius will involve humanitarian progress rather than be focussed on personal aspirations only. Your rebellious ideas and/or actions must lead to greater-than-personal results if they are ever to be accepted as valuable by others. Here, in Aquarius, you learn to recognize what's best for all rather than seeing things from a singular point of view only. Those having strong Aquarius traits are the inventors of our world. They move into the unknown in an attempt to find new directives for the future. Without such vision no social progress would ever occur. Your chart describes where you play a part in this pattern of change.

The keyphrase for Aquarius is "I KNOW." "I KNOW, without having any facts to prove that what I know is true." You need to move out on the basis of your intuitive vision and discover, or invent, something valuable, based on your visions. "I KNOW who I am regardless of what I have been taught to be. I KNOW these things, not because I have been taught that they are so, but because the knowledge is within me." In Aquarius your intuition is strong and much can be learned by listening to your inner voice and watching your visions unfold. Do you have the courage to act on your inner knowings, OR are you too afraid of what others might think? OR, are you afraid of the changes these truths might induce?

From a negative level, there is a tendency to go overboard in your desire to be independent and to break free from rigid rules. You could be an extremist. To rebel against obsolete structures is one thing, but to rebel for the sake of rebellion has only little value to the future. It is true that you are challenged to be different here, to dare to be unique, to dare to defy the odds if need be, BUT, before doing so be sure there is a good cause.

Leo lies opposite Aquarius in the zodiac, providing an important polarity, or balance. Leo is concerned with self-importance. Aquarius' concern must be for the good of the group. Without Aquarius to offer balance for Leo, too great an emphasis would be placed on the self. On the other hand, without Leo, Aquarius can appear cold or aloof in its commitment to the future, showing little concern for the needs of each individual within the larger community. In fact, there would be a tendency to lose oneself in a group cause. While the cause is important, self development is too.

The picture chosen to symbolize Aquarius is a man carrying a water pitcher, representing distilled wisdom being shared with the world. This is shown by the man pouring water (knowledge from the past) into the larger stream (the masses). Its glyph (♒) is often confusing, as it appears to some to be waves of water, while to others it represents streaks of lightning. While it is true that the Aquarian ideas may create "waves" when expressed to others, the image of lightning better describes the Aquarius purpose. As the darkest skies are illumined by lightning, so are our lives when we "tune into" the Aquarian message and dare to investigate our intuitive flashes.

When the urge to be unique and the need to break out of a mold you no longer fit into is ignored, Aquarius diseases could result. While Gemini deals with the nervous system in general, Aquarius rules the more highly attuned nervous system. Failure to express outwardly the highly excitable, yet original, qualities of Aquarius can turn in on itself, resulting in nervous disorders of a unique or rare type. Eccentric or erratic behavior is induced by stressful situations. Excessive rebellion, when left undirected, frequently results in unnecessary accidents. Aquarius also rules the ankles. The ankles enable the feet to move forward. When not moving in a forward direction, or if trying to move forward too rapidly, the ankles are strained as is the positive potential of this exceptionally creative sign.

Some keywords which can help you recall the messages of Aquarius include:

POSITIVE: original, inventive, progressive, reforming, group-aware.

NEGATIVE: eccentric, erratic, rebellious, cold, unconventional.

Aquarius provided mental images of the possibilities of a new tomorrow. You have seen potential trends for future living. You have broken away from an old way of life and are about to enter a new world. But, before doing so, one final test must be confronted, one final step must be taken which will bring you to the door of Pisces to ask . . .

"Is It Really Possible?"

PISCES

With the revelations met in Aquarius you meet a new challenge in the next sign, Pisces. Here, a total commitment must be made to proceed with what, until now, has been only a vision, but what could eventually become a reality. Commitment is the keynote here. In Pisces you are encouraged not just to LOOK into the unknown, as in Aquarius, but to WALK into the unknown even though there is no proof that what you seek could, or ever will, exist. No tangible substances will be here to prove that what you envision will ever take form. The unknown is calling. Are you willing to follow the voice? Your journey has been a long one and you may feel worn out when venturing into the experiences ruled by the last sign of the zodiac.

There is often difficulty focussing on the here and now when dealing with the affairs ruled by this house. Something vague and mysterious is happening here. You are contacting a force that goes beyond form, and this very force, be it your unconscious or God, is challenging you to make a commitment with faith, even if personal sacrifices must be made in the process. In Pisces you learn to see things beyond form. You learn to understand the intangibles of life and to develop an appreciation for that which goes beyond material worth, but rather involves spiritual value. This does not infer that you will not have material satisfaction here, but that you must learn to see beyond it.

The power of positive thinking, psychic abilities, unselfish love and a willingness to help when help is needed, even if personal sacrifices must sometimes be made, are all a part of the Pisces experience. But, with these qualities, there is also a need to develop the wisdom to know when it is time to stop giving and allow others to help themselves.

Personal ambitions and ego involvements must be put aside in Pisces in order to pursue the goals aroused through your Aquarius experiences. Your "cause" must have greater-than-personal significance if you are ever to find peace within yourself. Here, you are challenged to view yourself as a part of a larger whole. If you have followed the cycle of the signs creatively up until this point you have already secured your personal needs. Now it is time to define how you fit into not just your society from a practical point of view, but your world from an evolutionary perspective. Here you are challenged to give back to the universe what it has given you through the greatest gift of all--the gift of life.

The experiences met in the house of Pisces are often considered to be "karmic" in the sense that you are confronted with your past. If there are outstanding "debts" still pending you will confront them through the experiences attracted in your Pisces house. A new, more enlightened identity is about to emerge. But first, the debts of the past must be cleared. Aware that you are no longer a product of the past, but not yet a part of the future, you may feel as though you are hanging in a state of limbo.

The keyphrase for Pisces is "I BELIEVE." "I BELIEVE in the future and realize that if I am to progress I must make a commitment to my beliefs." This belief, however, must be cultivated as, at first, you might have fears connected with this area of your life. The faith required in Pisces must be built from experience. Seldom is it inherent in the nature.

In Pisces you learn to give. You must periodically return to your source to be reminded of the importance not only of your own existence, but of the importance of the existence of mankind as a whole. Whatever sacrifices are necessary to make in order to contribute to this larger whole are confronted.

The story of Jonathan Livingston Seagull exemplifies the meaning of Pisces very well. Jonathan expressed a strong Aquarian urge to break away from conditioned concepts of what a seagull could do. His family (strictly Capricornian) told him over and over again that he was a SEAGULL, and a seagull could not soar as could an eagle. Yet, something inside said to him: "Yes you can!" Was it a compulsion or an illumination?

"I KNOW I can," he said. "I KNOW and I BELIEVE. I will move out into the unknown at the risk of my own physical existence because I am totally committed to my belief." Jonathan proved to his family and peers that he could be more than what was expected of a seagull. He had faith. As he soared through the heavens he helped awaken others to potentials they had never recognized. Jonathan didn't lose, nor will you if your faith is strong. Based on your degree of faith and the human concern for social progress, you will, through your Pisces experiences, find either true inner peace and serenity or live in constant fear of loss.

Faith should not be confused, however, with escapism. It is easy to get caught up in a world of unreality in the Pisces house. When this happens, you are open to all kinds of negative invasions and "vibrations," unable to see truth from fiction. Not only could you become open to deceptive influences, you could easily fool yourself by closing your eyes to problems which never really go away. When a problem surfaces it seems easier to ignore it and escape from it rather than accepting it and working it through with love. Typical escape routes taken by Pisces include the misuse of drugs, alcohol, evasiveness or an attempt to live in a dream world. On the other hand, it is equally important that you don't allow yourself to be used as a "sponge" by others here, absorbing others' negative energy. The Virgo polarity can help you to avoid this tendency.

Virgo lies opposite Pisces, as illustrated on page 53. Virgo provides the ability to give discriminately. Without Virgo, Pisces tends to live in a dream world. There is a tendency either to give or to receive services indiscriminately. Virgo acts as a reminder that God helps those who help themselves. No individual is another's savior. We may only contribute to another's salvation. At the same time, Virgo needs Pisces to soften its critical tendencies. Pisces helps you to view things from a larger, more compassionate dimension rather than getting caught up in the details of living.

For the picture chosen to represent Pisces, you will find two fish, each swimming in opposite directions but bound together with a band. One fish represents evolution while the other signifies involution. Its glyph (♓) can also be seen as two fish. From another perspective it is two half moons, one representing the conscious mind, while the other represents the unconscious. The bar between the two symbolizes the "missing link" which is capable of uniting these two seemingly separate halves.

With faith as a foundation in your Pisces activities you will stand tall. Lack of faith weakens the foundations, as represented by Pisces' rulership over the feet. If you have problems with your feet maybe it's time to examine the strength of your faith in the matters ruled by your Pisces house. Fears, doubts, past failures which haunt you, when left unresolved, can fester until they weaken the strength of your base.

The creative, yet evasive, tendency of Pisces can also result in an obsession with and extreme sensitivity to drugs. Altering the psychic balance through unnatural means creates distortion and eventually dissolves the spiritual, psychological and physical foundations upon which your life stands. If you suffer from Pisces diseases maybe it's time to review your life in terms of your spiritual faith. Try making this year one of compassion, giving without expectation, serving without losing your ego and believing that tomorrow's Sun will shine even if today's weather has been foggy.

Some keywords to help you remember the essence of Pisces include:

POSITIVE: idealistic, spiritual, sensitive, giving, compassionate, psychic.

NEGATIVE: escapism, wishy-washy, fearful, unrealistic.

A Pause to Reflect

As you reach the end of your journey through the signs and houses of the birth chart you soon find that your expedition is not over, but only again just about to begin. As you face the past in Pisces (the same sign requiring a commitment to the future), you realize that you are about to begin anew, in Aries, with a new identity, a new value system (Taurus), new appreciation for knowledge (Gemini), new foundations providing security (Cancer), a new sense of self-importance and purpose (Leo), new appreciation for detail and its importance (Virgo), new attitudes about sharing (Libra), attitudes still needing transformation (Scorpio), a new understanding of philosophy and life (Sagittarius), a new social territory yet to be claimed (Capricorn). There are new visions of what still lies ahead (Aquarius) which require new faith and commitment to continue your growth (Pisces).

The cycle is a never ending one. Each day it is completed at some level, even though we are not conscious of its unfoldment. As you move on to experience the planets, you will find KEYS which will help you to see what must be done in order to insure this unfoldment is creative.

Intercepted Signs

You may notice that certain signs in your chart do not occupy house CUSPS but have been placed, instead, in the middle of a house between other signs located on the actual house cusps. These signs are called "intercepted" or "captured." A whole book has been written about these very important signs in your chart and I refer you to it for more in-depth information. (*Intercepted Signs, Environment vs Destiny*, by Joanne Wickenburg.) However, before reading further, you should be alerted to the basic implications suggested by signs in an intercepted condition in the birth chart.

Once again, remember that houses deal with external areas of life. The house CUSPS represent the DOORS leading into these various life experiences. The signs on the cusps, or doors, represent your basic orientation toward each department of life. As you will find later in this book, planets ruling these signs represent the "keys" which enable you to unlock and enter into the experiences each house rules. BUT, when a sign is intercepted, it has no doorway through which to meet the outer experiences which enhance its expression and utilize its potential. This does not mean that these signs are not useful or expressed in your life, but it does suggest that OUTER conditions—environmental facilities—are not immediately available to help you fulfill the needs or develop the potentials they provide. In essence, you must find your answers within yourself rather than looking outside for assistance in developing these talents and capabilities.

While intercepted signs do create frustration due to the lack of cooperation or encouragement available in your surroundings, they by no means must indicate handicaps or repressions. There are often delays involved with fulfilling the needs they represent due to the lack of outer stimuli. However, because they must be developed and fulfilled through personal, subjective, soul-searching experiences, they can become unique in their final expression as they are not conditioned by external influences.

First Studies of Chart Synthesis

As previously mentioned, there is a similarity between signs and the houses to which they correspond numerically (Aries/1st house, Taurus/2nd house, Gemini/3rd house, Cancer/4th house, etc.). Once you begin to understand the significance of this relationship, you are ready to begin learning the art of chart synthesis.

The signs, in themselves, can only be viewed in the abstract until they are associated with the experiences of the houses. When the two are considered in combination, their astrological significance becomes personal, relative to your life specifically rather than as a cyclic pattern pertaining to mankind as a whole. Likewise, houses show only external circumstances which cannot be personally defined without viewing them in relation to the signs. The degree of development of one is dependent on the other, as you will see when reading further.

In the following, you will find how the signs and their corresponding houses are interpreted when seen in relation to an actual birth chart. However, these descriptions are based on NEEDS rather than actual fact or circumstance. Whether the needs are easily fulfilled or the projection of the signs are positive or negative depends on factors not yet discussed. Realize also that this relationship cannot be determined without an actual birth chart constructed from the date, time and place of birth.

Aries/First House

You discover, through the experiences described by the house on which you find Aries, your capacity for independent living. Here, you need to move into new experiences courageously in order to develop your identity. As a result, you become aware of your ability to do your own thing without depending on others. You discover, through self-proving initiative, your separateness.

The identity, however, is not DEFINED, or characterized, by the sign, Aries. You may not PROJECT your identity in typical Arian fashion (assertively, impulsively, daringly, forcefully). In order to describe the manner with which you project your identity you must look to the sign on your 1st house cusp, or the Ascendant. In other words, as you develop an independent, self-proving attitude and a pioneering approach to the experiences described by Aries' house, your self-image and the outer projection of your identity becomes more and more positive. Until the Aries house has been explored, however, the negative aspects of the Ascendant sign are likely to be projected. When seen in general terms, Aries represents the identity—the ability to see yourself as separate from others—while the first house sign describes the MANIFESTATION of that identity. Whether the projection of your identity is positive or negative depends largely on the degree of courage you use to forge continually ahead into new experiences in the house of Aries.

Following, you will find brief descriptions for each possible combination involving Aries and the 1st house sign. The technique established here can be used when assessing all signs and their natural houses as two units in a very important partnership.

Aries on 2nd House/Pisces on 1st

Once you "find" yourself by learning to handle material responsibilities independently and take the initiative to acquire life sustaining requirements on your own (Aries on 2nd house), you are encouraged to use your strengths and PROJECT your resourcefulness in a manner which welcomes the unknown and demonstrates true concern for others (Pisces on 1st). Until you have become aware, through action, of your own resourcefulness and strength (Aries on 2nd), others see you as an escapist, approaching life with fear, expecting others to take care of you (negative Pisces).

Aries on 2nd House/Aquarius on 1st

Once you "find" yourself by learning to handle material responsibilities independently and take the initiative to acquire life sustaining requirements on your own (Aries on 2nd house), you are encouraged to use your strengths and PRO-

JECT your resourcefulness in a manner which is unique, original, future-oriented and concerned for humanity's welfare in progress (Aquarius on 1st). Until you have become aware, through action, of your resourcefulness and strength (Aries on 2nd), others see you as a rebel, having no real foundation for your rebellion (negative Aquarius).

Aries on 3rd House/Aquarius on 1st

Once you "find" yourself by daring to investigate new ideas, being an independent thinker and looking beyond the obvious for information (Aries on 3rd house), you are encouraged to PROJECT your intellectuality in a manner which is unique, unconditioned by society, progressive and future-oriented (Aquarius on 1st). Until you have become aware, through action, of your intellectuality and have acted on your ideas (Aries on 3rd), others see you as a rebel, having no real foundation for your rebellion (negative Aquarius).

Aries on 3rd House/Capricorn on 1st

Once you "find" yourself by daring to investigate new ideas, being an independent thinker and looking beyond the obvious for information (Aries on 3rd house), you are encouraged to PROJECT your intellectuality in a manner which is well-organized, structured, socially acceptable and responsible (Capricorn on 1st). Until you have become aware, through action, of your intellectuality and have acted on your ideas (Aries on 3rd), others see you as overly rigid, authoritarian and somewhat pessimistic (negative Capricorn).

Aries on 3rd House/Sagittarius on 1st

Once you "find" yourself by daring to investigate new ideas, being an independent thinker and looking beyond the obvious for information (Aries on 3rd house), you are encouraged to PROJECT your intellectuality in a manner which is open-minded, philosophical and goal-oriented (Sagittarius on 1st). Until you have become aware, through action, of your intellectuality and have acted on your ideas (Aries on 3rd), others see you as unreliable, failing to practice what you preach, somewhat vague or fanatical in opinion (negative Sagittarius).

Aries on 4th House/Capricorn on 1st

Once you "find" yourself by independently securing your life's foundations, proving to yourself that you can stand alone if need be and still be secure (Aries on 4th house), you are encouraged to PROJECT your well-grounded self in a manner which is practical, well-organized, territory-aware and responsible (Capricorn on 1st). Until you have secured your foundations through independent action (Aries on 4th), others see you as overly rigid, authoritarian and somewhat pessimistic (negative Capricorn).

Aries on 4th House/Sagittarius on 1st

Once you "find" yourself by independently securing your life's foundations, proving to yourself that you can stand alone if need be and still be secure (Aries on 4th house), you are encouraged to PROJECT your well-grounded self in a manner which is expansive, philosophical, open minded and goal-oriented (Sagittarius on 1st). Until you have secured your foundations through independent action (Aries on 4th), others see you as unrealiable, vague, failing to practice what you preach or fanatical in opinion (negative Sagittarius).

Aries on 5th House/Sagittarius on 1st

Once you "find" yourself through your creations, pioneering new areas of self-expression and seeing a part of yourself reflected in all that you create (Aries on 5th house), you are encouraged to PROJECT your creative self in a manner which is open-minded, philosophical, expansive and goal-oriented (Sagittarius on 1st). Until you prove to yourself, through action, that you are creative (Aries on 5th), others see you as unreliable, vague, failing to practice what you preach or fanatical in opinion (negative Sagittarius).

Aries on 5th House/Scorpio on 1st

Once you "find" yourself through your creations, pioneering new areas of self-expression and seeing a part of yourself reflected through what you have created (Aries on 5th house), you are encouraged to PROJECT your creativity in a manner which is intense, regenerating and expressing depth in character (Scorpio on 1st). Until you have proven to yourself, through action, that you are creative (Aries on 5th), others see you as controlling, suspicious, jealous or destructive (negative Scorpio).

Aries on 6th House/Scorpio on 1st

Once you "find" yourself by becoming independently useful in a daily routine, proving to yourself, through action, that you are responsible at a daily level (Aries on 6th house), you are encouraged to PROJECT your organized self in a manner which is intense, regenerating and expressing depth in character (Scorpio on 1st). Until you prove your ability to be useful at a daily level and live up to the responsibilities required of you (Aries on 6th), others see you as controlling, suspicious, jealous or destructive (negative Scorpio).

Aries on 6th House/Libra on 1st

Once you "find" yourself by becoming independently useful within your daily routine, proving to yourself, through action, that you can be responsible at a daily level (Aries on 6th house), you are encouraged to PROJECT your organized self in a manner which is cooperative, sharing and shows true concern for others (Libra on 1st). Until you have proven to yourself, through action, your ability to be independently useful at a daily level and have lived up to the responsibilities required of you (Aries on 6th), others see you as manipulating, indecisive or a leaner (negative Libra).

Aries on 7th House/Libra on 1st

Once you "find" yourself through the relationships you attract and understand your separate role within them (Aries on 7th house), you are encouraged to PROJECT your newfound objectivity in a manner which is cooperative, sharing and shows true concern for others (Libra on 1st). Until you find yourself through relationships and the feedback they offer, understanding the individual role you must play within them (Aries on 7th), others see you as manipulating, indecisive or a leaner (negative Libra).

Aries on 8th House/Virgo on 1st

Once you "find" yourself by initiating changes and making the sacrifices necessary to maintain relationships (Aries on 8th house), you are encouraged to PROJECT your ever-regenerating identity in a manner which is discriminating, analytical and aware of the details that go into making anything successful (Virgo on 1st). Until you have taken the initiative to make necessary changes in your life, taken steps to regenerate your ego and to understand the depths of your being (Aries on 8th), others see you as overly critical, nit-picking and trapped in detail rather than appreciative of it (negative Virgo).

Aries on 8th House/Libra on 1st

Once you "find" yourself by initiating changes and making the sacrifices necessary to maintain relationships (Aries on 8th house), you are encouraged to PROJECT your ever-regenerating identity in a manner which is cooperative, sharing and shows genuine concern for others (Libra on 1st). Until you have taken the initiative to make changes in your life, taken steps to regenerate your ego and to understand the depths of your being (Aries on 8th), others see you as indecisive, a manipulator or a leaner (negative Libra).

Aries on 9th House/Leo on 1st

Once you "find" yourself by daring to look beyond your own environment, gathering new experiences and insights about other cultures or philosophies and have acquired a broad-range education in general (Aries on 9th house), you are encouraged to PROJECT your broad-minded self in a manner which shows confidence, is dramatic and exhibits strength of character (Leo on 1st). Until you have looked further than your own back yard for knowledge and have pioneered into progressive philosophical thought (Aries on 9th), others see you as overly proud, domineering or egotistical in your approach to life (negative Leo).

Aries on 9th House/Virgo on 1st

Once you "find" yourself by daring to look beyond your own environment, gathering new experiences and insights about other cultures or philosophies and have acquired a broad range education (Aries on 9th house), you are encouraged to PROJECT your mentally expansive self in a manner which is discriminating, analytical and aware of the details that go into making anything meaningful (Virgo on 1st). Until you have looked further than your own back yard for knowledge and have pioneered into progressive philosophical thought (Aries on 9th), others see you as overly critical, nit-picking and trapped in detail rather than appreciative of it (negative Virgo).

Aries on 10th House/Cancer on 1st

Once you "find" yourself by independently venturing into the professional world, accepting social responsibilities and understanding your role in successes and failures (Aries on 10th house), you are encouraged to PROJECT your public stand, or title, in a manner which is sensitive, nurturing and security-providing (Cancer on 1st). Until you have independently taken steps to achieve success in a public sense and proven your ability to function independently at a social level (Aries on 10th), others see you as moody, clinging and insecure in your approach to life (negative Cancer).

Aries on 10th House/Leo on 1st

Once you "find" yourself by independently venturing into the professional world, accepting social responsibilities and understanding your role in successes and failures (Aries on 10th house), you are encouraged to PROJECT your public stand, or title, in a manner which expresses confidence, is dramatic and shows strength of character (Leo on 1st). Until you have independently taken steps to achieve success and proven your ability to function at a social level (Aries on 10th), others see you as overly-proud, domineering or egotistical in your approach to life (negative Leo).

Aries on 11th House/Gemini on 1st

Once you "find" yourself by taking the initiative to meet others and have accepted a leadership role with friends or in groups, expressing your progressive self (Aries on 11th house), you are encouraged to PROJECT your social self in a manner which is curious, communicative, versatile and intelligent (Gemini on 1st). Until you have become socially assertive and developed the courage to move toward the future independently (Aries on 11th), others see you as superficial, changeable, scattered or shallow (negative Gemini).

Aries on 11th House/Cancer on 1st

Once you "find" yourself by taking the initiative to meet others, taking on a leadership role with friends or in groups, expressing your progressive ideas (Aries on 11th house), you are encouraged to PROJECT your social self in a manner which is sensitive, nurturing, warm and security-providing (Cancer on 1st). Until you have become socially assertive and developed the courage to move toward the future independently (Aries on 11th), others see you as insecure, moody or dependent on outside circumstances (negative Cancer).

Aries on 12th House/Taurus on 1st

Once you "find" yourself by getting out of yourself enough to see your individual role in the larger scheme of things, transcending selfish desires and independently handling old "debts" (Aries on 12th house), you are encouraged to PROJECT your selfless self in a manner which is practical, sense-aware, resourceful and determined (Taurus on 1st). Until you have independently taken steps to overcome past limitations and have given to others with love rather than expectation (Aries on 12th), others see you as stubborn, materialistic, dogmatic or lazy (negative Taurus).

Aries on 1st House

This is what is called a "natural" chart as the first sign, Aries, occupies the first house of the chart. You "find" yourself by moving into life with courage, daring to be independent and proving to yourself, through action, that you can function on your own (Aries on 1st house). Then, you are encouraged to PROJECT your self-found identity in a manner which is pioneering, forward moving, self assertive and fearless (Aries on 1st). Until you have found creative techniques for moving into new experiences on your own, having developed courage in your own abilities (Aries on 1st), others see you as headstrong, self involved, combative or augumentative (negative Aries).

Aries Intercepted 1st House/Pisces on 1st

Once you "find" yourself by moving into life with courage, daring to be independent and proving to yourself, through action, that you can function on your own (Aries in 1st house), you are encouraged to PROJECT your self-found identity in a manner which welcomes the unknown and demonstrates true concern for others, willing to give when help is needed (Pisces on 1st). Until you have found creative techniques for moving into new experiences on your own, having developed courage in your own abilities (Aries in 1st), others see you approaching life with fear, expecting others to take care of you or living a life of illusion (negative Pisces).

Taurus/Second House

Through your Taurus-ruled activities (house), you learn to be resourceful. Your approach to these matters must be based on the potential worth or value of your actions. Here, you learn to be practical and down to earth in order to maintain your life at a physical, mental, material and spiritual level. Survival is the keynote of Taurus. To determine the MANIFESTATION of your productive efforts, once functioning within the environment, refer to the sign on your 2nd house cusp. While Taurus' house shows where you need to be resourceful, the sign on the 2nd house describes the TYPES of strengths or talents which must be cultivated in order to maintain a productive life.

EXAMPLE: Taurus on 5th house/Aquarius on 2nd.
There is a need to use your creative potential in a practical manner in order to produce something tangible (Taurus on 5th). Then, use these creative products in a unique, progressive, unconditioned and original manner in order to acquire tangible assets required for survival (Aquarius on 2nd).

In summary . . .

TAURUS . . . where (house) you need to be resourceful.

2ND HOUSE . . . the nature (sign) of your resourcefulness.

Gemini/Third House

The house of Gemini describes an area of life providing intellectual stimulation. Here, curiosity urges you to investigate new concepts. You learn to be adaptable, to accept new ideas and to investigate mental mysteries. Through the options available in Gemini's house you learn to make choices, to ask questions and to communicate with others. Gemini's house, however, does not DEFINE your approach to learning experiences nor does it describe the environmental facilities available for learning. The latter is a 3rd house matter. Your approach to, and needs regarding, learning facilities in your community are described by the sign on your 3rd house cusp. While Gemini shows where knowledge is available and where questions are posed which arouse curiosity, the sign on the 3rd house cusp describes your individual approach to these learning experiences once functioning in the world around you.

EXAMPLE: Gemini on 11th house/Libra on 3rd.
Friends and group involvements arouse curiosity concerning new possibilities for learning and investigation into mysteries yet unexplored (Gemini on 11th house). The manner with which you can best fulfill this curiosity via outside learning facilities is through one-to-one contacts with others which involve sharing of ideas and provide objectivity through feedback (Libra on 3rd).

In summary . . .

GEMINI . . . where (house) curiosity stimulates the intellect.

3RD HOUSE . . . available learning facilities and your basic approach to them (sign).

Cancer/Fourth House

Cancer's house describes a department of life where you need security. You need to express and experience human warmth when dealing with this area of your life. Here, you give and receive emotional support by building protective boundaries. Yet, while the house of Cancer shows where security is needed, it does not describe the nature of your emotional foundations. This is the role of the 4th house sign. The types of foundations needed for secure living are described by the sign on your 4th house. The degree of security gained by operating within secure boundaries in Cancer's house determines the solidity of your 4th house base. Requirements regarding personal "grounding" are described by the sign on your 4th house cusp.

EXAMPLE: Cancer on 6th house/Taurus on 4th.
You need to feel secure with the routine conditions of your life, including work and the definition of daily responsibility (Cancer on 6th). The degree to which security is established in the daily routine determines whether or not personal foundations are secure at a tangible level (Taurus on 4th).

In summary . . .

CANCER . . . where (house) personal security is needed.

4TH HOUSE . . . the nature (sign) of your emotional foundations.

Leo/Fifth House

While the house of Leo shows where you need to feel purposeful and personally creative, the sign on the 5th house cusp describes the nature of your creative expressions once projected outwardly. The 5th house sign describes how your creative ideas can best be utilized and the form they take. Here, you find and define your creative potential in order to prepare a legacy which will live on after you have gone. As your children are a part of this legacy, the 5th house also describes your approach to rearing your young.

EXAMPLE: Leo on 9th house/Gemini on 5th.
The need to approach higher learning and philosophical concepts (9th house) with purposeful direction and to use the essence of your wisdom to build confidence (Leo). Then, you need to develop an intellectual mode for creatively communicating this purpose (Gemini on 5th).

In summary . . .

LEO . . . where (house) you discover your importance.

5TH HOUSE . . . how (sign) you express your purpose outwardly.

Virgo/Sixth House

Virgo's house shows where you learn to handle routine responsibilities. Here, you develop analytical skills as you strive to perfect those things proven to be inadequate for practical, daily use. Toward the experiences ruled by Virgo's house you are critical, discriminating and always aware of detail. While Virgo shows where, by house, you learn to handle routine, it does not describe the approach you take when pursuing daily chores. Virgo encourages you to be useful, while the sign on the 6th house cusp describes the best methods to use when performing routine tasks and the types of daily responsibilities and services you will confront.

EXAMPLE: Virgo on 3rd/Sagittarius on 6th.
You need to find practical means for applying knowledge through environmental facilities and to be discriminating concerning information input (Virgo on 3rd house). Then, apply that information in your routine working life with an expansive, futuristic attitude (Sagittarius on 6th).

In summary . . .

VIRGO . . . where (house) you learn to handle routine and schedule your time.

6TH HOUSE . . . the type (sign) of routine experienced at a daily level.

Libra/Seventh House

In the house of Libra you need relationships which offer feedback and alternative viewpoints. Here you learn to cooperate, you develop objectivity by seeing how your ideas are received by others and by listening to what others offer in return. While Libra shows where you need relationships, it does not describe the types of relationships which can best offer the kind of feedback needed. This is the role of the 7th house sign. Here, in the 7th house, you find the types of people who can help you balance your life. The characteristics of the sign on this cusp are foreign to you until you attract others who bring them to the surface.

EXAMPLE: Libra on 9th house/Cancer on 7th.
There is an urge to share philosophies and visions with others to get feedback (Libra on 9th). These relationships bring out your maternal, nurturing instincts and sensitivity in dealing with others (Cancer on 7th).

In summary . . .

LIBRA . . . where (house) you need relationships which develop other-awareness.

7TH HOUSE . . . the types (sign) of relationships encouraging objectivity.

Scorpio/Eighth House

Through the experiences met in the house ruled by Scorpio, the process of regeneration begins. Here, you become intensely involved with what surrounds you and, as a result, come to realize the importance of changing the patterns which prohibit further involvement. While the house of Scorpio shows where change or regeneration is needed, it does not define attitudes needing adjustment, nor does it define the manner with which you meet life's changes. The latter can be found by looking to the sign on the 8th house cusp. The 8th house sign describes how you approach life's changes and defines personality characteristics which must be regenerated in order to maintain all types of relationships. In your 8th house, personal sacrifices must be made in order to find a deeper meaning to your life. Here, the ego goes through a rebirth.

EXAMPLE: Scorpio on 10th house/Virgo on 8th.
Awareness of the need to change your life from a strictly ego-centered point of view manifests through career involvements and society's reactions to your social accomplishments (Scorpio on 10th). The need to be deeply involved with professional activities and goals induces regeneration (Scorpio on 10th). The approach taken to the changes deemed necessary is analytical, discriminating, organized and critical (Virgo on 8th). At the same time, the tendency to be excessively critical in times of change must be worked through.

In summary . . .

SCORPIO . . . where (house) regeneration is experienced.

8TH HOUSE . . . how (sign) the need for life's changes is confronted.

Sagittarius/Ninth House

In Sagittarius you set goals for the future. You broaden your horizons through the expansive avenues of activity available in its house. As you expand foundations, you develop a larger point of view and formulate a philosophy by which to live. The nature of your philosophical beliefs is described by the sign on the 9th house cusp. Your approach to higher learning, religious matters or travel which enhances your understanding of cultural differences or foreign thought is shown by the 9th house sign.

EXAMPLE: Sagittarius on 6th house/Pisces on 9th.
Through expansive experiences encountered at a daily level in work or other routine activity you broaden your outlook on life and develop a philosophy by which to live (Sagittarius on 6th). The nature of this philosophy and your approach to higher learning is universal rather than orthodox, based on faith rather than fact and calls for a personal commitment (Pisces on 9th).

In summary . . .

SAGITTARIUS . . . where (house) you broaden your horizons and develop a larger viewpoint.

9TH HOUSE . . . how (sign) you perceive higher laws and approach extensive learning experiences.

Capricorn/Tenth House

In Capricorn you need to build foundations which give you a sense of social belongingness. You need to be respected for your social accomplishments. The house of Capricorn describes where you learn to live within limits, to define your social territory as separate from that of others and to defend that territory if need be. Your social "place" is described by the sign on your 10th house cusp. Here, you find what needs are prominent when choosing a vocational direction, your basic approach to success and career, and the nature of your social or vocational reputation.

EXAMPLE: Capricorn on 2nd house/Virgo on 10th.
You need to use your resources within practical limits and to define, in specific terms, your capacity to be productive. You need to understand where your territory begins and ends when it comes to spending money or using your energy (Capricorn on 2nd). Your social reputation will be based on

your ability to organize, handle detail and criticize to improve what already exists (Virgo on 10th).

In summary . . .

CAPRICORN . . . where (house) you need to define your role in a social sense.

10TH HOUSE . . . the nature (sign) of your social involvements and the basis of your reputation.

Aquarius/Eleventh House

In Aquarius you experience an urge to break free from social limitations, to begin exploring ideas and experiences which were not a part of your conditioning process. Here, you discover your capacity to be unique, original and inventive. You find that you can be more than what you were taught to be. As a result of the awareness brought on by the Aquarius experience, you begin to define new goals for the future. These goals are described by the sign on your 11th house cusp. Your approach to friends and groups which encourage progress is also found here.

EXAMPLE: Aquarius on 1st house/Sagittarius on 11th.
As a result of independent ventures into new experiences, you develop a unique, progressive, humanitarian outlook on life (Aquarius on 1st). You learn to set goals for the future. These goals are philosophical and open-ended, encouraged by friends and groups who share your vision. Through such contacts you expand your understanding of life and its future possibilities (Sagittarius on 11th).

In summary . . .

AQUARIUS . . . where (house) you break free from limitations to discover your originality and uniqueness.

11TH HOUSE . . . the types (sign) of goals you look forward to and the kinds of people you attract as friends.

Pisces/Twelfth House

The house of Pisces encourages you to let go of past security dependencies and make a commitment to the future, even though there are no clear signs or promises that what you envision will ever take form. Faith is required here. When functioning in this area of your life you need willingly to make sacrifices in order to contribute to the needs of others. The approach best taken to voluntary services is described by the sign on the 12th house cusp. The nature of the commitment made in Pisces is described by the 12th house sign. Personal debts which must be confronted and handled in the 12th house experience are described by the sign on its cusp.

EXAMPLE: Pisces on 4th house/Scorpio on 12th.
There is a need to dissolve old security dependencies and build foundations on faith rather than form (Pisces on 4th). As faith is developed, you are encouraged to contribute to the larger whole of humanity and to recognize your oneness with all. You need to transcend a tendency to be controlling and become intensely involved with services and your commitment to the future (Scorpio on 12th).

In summary . . .

PISCES . . . where (house) you are tested according to your faith in the unknown and become conscious of your oneness with mankind.

12TH HOUSE . . . the nature (sign) of your potential services and what needs to be transcended in order to feel secure in giving.

The Planets

Planets, unlike signs, deal with specific personality energies or functions. The planets illustrate the actual drama of your life, describing, by house, where the action is and defining, by sign, its nature. The relationship between signs, houses and planets is worth repeating:

SIGNS show attitudes and needs. They do NOT describe activity taking place.

HOUSES describe areas of life. They have NO personality characteristics until seen in relation to the signs.

SIGNS ON HOUSES describe basic attitudes and needs (signs) regarding external living (houses).

PLANETS, on the other hand, describe the types of energies, based on their degree of development, required to fulfill the needs of the signs within the areas of life defined by the houses in which they are located.

Each planet "rules" a specific sign(s), as each planet describes a type of action necessary to fulfill the needs of a particular sign(s). Therefore, it is important to view planets, not just singularly in terms of energy-representatives, but according to their sign rulership.

The Sun

The Sun's house describes where you become conscious of your purpose and the importance of your existence. Here, you find where your purpose lies. The sign describes how this purpose can best be developed. As the Sun rules Leo, the degree of consciousness gained via its exposure will determine the quality of self-expression projected through your Leo-ruled house.

The Sun, center of our solar system, represents the inner you--your inner will which is separate from the social ego and carries the purpose of the higher self. It illuminates, enlightens, or makes conscious the importance of doing something purposeful within the experiences described by the house it occupies, so that you feel positive about your life. Where you find your Sun (house), there you discover your potential to shine in some way. Through the Sun's experiences you develop consciousness and life direction, the level of which determines the true importance of what you are living out in your Leo house.

By developing your Sun potential you gain personal dignity and self respect. You begin to integrate your life. You become the "pilot of your own ship." If you do not consciously develop the area of life described by its house, and find a sense of purpose within it, you could be easily ruled by outer conditions or allow unconscious compulsions to rule you. Lacking dignity, having no true direction, you could become disoriented to the degree that life itself seems out of focus. Over-compensation for your lack of self esteem could be demonstrated through domineering or egotistical projections or, at the other extreme, an inability to exert your will.

While the Ascendant, or Rising Sign, describes the outer you (the personality you show to the world), the Sun's sign describes the inner you—the inner power of your personality or, if not developed, your inner weaknesses. Whether the Sun sign is apt to be expressed positively or negatively can only be determined by the Sun's relationship to the other planets in your chart. This relationship (aspects) will be discussed in a later chapter.

The Moon

The Moon represents emotional responses and habits. Its house describes an area of life where emotions are aroused while its sign defines the nature of your emotional responses. Not really a planet, but a satellite of the earth, the Moon revolves around the earth at a much faster rate than do the planets in their geocentric orbits. Because of its more rapid transit, the Moon is responsible for daily changes of mood and circumstance which test your degree of adaptability.

The house containing the Moon describes the area of life where changes are most frequently experienced. These changes are not abrupt or dramatic, but can cause emotional stress if ignored. The Moon's sign describes how you react to emotional situations based on past experiences which have conditioned those responses, particularly those involving your early relationship with your mother. In fact, the Moon defines a quality (sign) you have inherited from, or one conditioned by, the mother. While not necessarily designating her "sign," it does describe a quality she projected (positive or negative) that has had a powerful influence on your degree of emotional stability.

As the Moon's sign describes responses and habits based on past experiences, it can easily become a negative factor in the chart if not integrated with the qualities of the Sun, which provides growth in consciousness. When seen in combination, the Sun shows how to use the experiences gained from the past (Moon) at a conscious, more progressive level. When not integrated with the solar energy, the Moon describes, by house, where you cling to memories of the past to the degree that you eventually lose sight of future potentials.

As ruler of Cancer, the Moon shows where adaptability is needed in order to maintain security in Cancer's house. In other words, while security is needed in the house of Cancer, you must work through the Moon by remaining adaptable to the changes experienced within the activities of its house, breaking out of obsolete responses and habits, in order to acquire it.

Mercury

Mercury's function is to accumulate information and factual data. It enables you to function on the basis of reason and logic rather than according to emotion and mood. Through Mercury's gift you develop the intellect. The sign containing Mercury at birth describes how you accumulate information and communicate data. Its house points to an area of life requiring thought and reason. In essence, Mercury represents the concrete, rational mind. It provides communicative skills and an ability to acquire data needed to develop through your Gemini experiences.

Ruler of two signs, Gemini and Virgo, Mercury's role is to gather information which fulfills your Gemini-need for learning. Then, to transmit that information into the Virgo experiences of your life where it is analyzed, criticized, seen according to its practical value, sorted and digested until what has been proven superfluous is eliminated while that having value is retained. Without Mercury your Gemini-questions will remain unanswered. Your thirst for information will go unquenched. Likewise, without Mercury no information will be available for criticism or utilization in Virgo's house experiences.

You could say: The 3rd house provides the school and the text books. The sign on its cusp describes these facilities and your approach and needs regarding them. Gemini introduces a personal need to acquire information and a desire to communicate with others. Virgo offers judgement and a filing system for information once received. The 6th house provides the external routine working responsibilities and facilities which require mental productivity and organization. HOWEVER, you must use Mercury, your mind, to do the actual learning, to ask the actual questions, to make the actual associations if any of the above are to be meaningful or fulfilling experiences.

Venus

Venus is your magnet; your power to attract. Through Venus you develop an appreciation for life at both a physical and social level. This is the planet of love. Without the potential to attract and to love, humanity would function in a purely mechanical manner. Venus provides experiences which cultivate self love and then, love for others. Like Mercury, it functions at two levels and therefore rules two astrological signs, Taurus and Libra.

Through its relationship to Taurus, Venus develops an appreciation for the tangible substances of life. The need for resources which guarantee survival, brought to your attention in Taurus, must depend on Venus for support. Venus stimulates an appreciation for your own worth. It encourages you to ask: What did you do for yourself today? By cultivating an appreciation and love for yourself you are inviting survival and success. Through Libra, Venus helps you to cultivate an appreciation for others. Within the experiences provided in Venus' house you attract people who stimulate both the receiving and giving of love. Its sign describes your receptivity to matters of the heart.

Venus rules the female gender in general. Its glyph is used in medical references to symbolize women. In a woman's chart, Venus describes, by sign, how she feels about her own femininity. Its house describes the experiences which help her to develop an appreciation for her sex. In a man's chart, Venus describes, by sign, the type of women to whom he is attracted. Women of this quality encourage him to express his own feminine/receptive characteristics.

Experiences which stimulate an appreciation for living are described by the house containing Venus. The degree to which you recognize the value of these experiences will determine the quality of what, and who, you attract from the outside. If solid values are not developed through the experiences of Venus' house you will attract people and conditions which are out of harmony with what you inwardly want or appreciate. In essence, others objectify your degree of self worth and concern for people in general.

Mars

Mars represents the urge for action, the desire to be direct, and your capacity for independence. Its sign describes how you assert yourself, while its house describes an area of life requiring, and therefore encouraging, independent, assertive, self-motivated action.

While Venus deals with receptive urges, Mars rules the aggressive instincts. It represents pure masculine energy, aggressive drive, animal instinct. In a man's chart, Mars, by sign, describes how he expresses and projects his masculinity, how he feels about his masculine gender. On the other hand, in a woman's chart Mars describes the type of men to whom she is drawn. The characteristics of this sign, as expressed through the men in her life, bring out her own aggressive, physical urges. Like two electrical currents, when Mars and Venus are seen as partners between men and women, sparks fly. This concept, however, refers not only to male/female relationships. The attractions brought out between the two need not be sexual. Basically, Venus describes what you want to attract in another to fulfill your receptive urges while Mars describes the physical approach you take to the attractions Venus stimulates.

As ruler of Aries, Mars represents the action required to fulfill your Aries-need for independence. The identity search beginning in Aries can only be initiated through actions stimulated by Mars. Aries describes an area of life (house) where you need to prove your existence and capacity to be independent. However, in order to do so, you must apply the courageous energy of Mars to put the desire into action. Mars also rules Scorpio. Here, the desires of Mars are regenerated as a result of outer, social contacts and involvements which require a less selfish, more intense expression of self. The house containing Mars shows an experience which once helped you to "find" yourself, but one which must be periodically reexamined and regenerated in order to maintain harmonious relationships.

As an example of Mars in its relationship to both Aries and Scorpio, consider a small child learning to walk. In the exuberance and inexperience of his first step no one is concerned if he steps on another's toes or knocks things over. However, once having gained confidence and skill in the art of walking, he must be more considerate. Thus, the original self involvement necessary in Mars' rulership of Aries must be tempered once you begin to function through the social signs.

Jupiter

♃

It is interesting to note the symbolism of the planets in comparison to their physical structure or appearance. It has been determined that Venus, for example, actually is magnetic, attracting debris from the solar system. In astrological interpretation, Venus provides the potential to attract substances and relationships. Mars, the red planet, provides energy and can be warlike in expression just as the color, red, is associated with passion and vitality. Jupiter, on the other hand, is the largest planet in our solar system. It isn't surprising to find the function of Jupiter involving the process of human expansion. Jupiter's function not only enables you to expand socially, spiritually, physically and mentally, but also operates as a magnifying force. It enlarges experiences, enhances understanding, but can also lead to self indulgence if its expansive urges are not curbed.

Jupiter's house describes an area of life where you meet experiences which offer an opportunity to expand your life, while its sign describes the manner in which this expansion takes place. If in a fire sign, for example, Jupiter encourages expansion through inspiration; in earth, material expansion. If in an air sign, it provides expansion at an intellectual level, while when in water, it expands emotional involvement.

Jupiter has always been considered to be a "fortunate" planet. It encourages promotion and enables you to broaden your scope of understanding due to the opportunities it provides. Based on these characteristics, you have probably already concluded that Jupiter rules Sagittarius. In the house of Sagittarius you discover a need for activities which enlarge your understanding of life. Through the experiences available in Jupiter's house this need can be met and fulfilled. Jupiter encourages you to move beyond the limitations of your environment, either mentally or physically. This broadening of experience brings fulfillment to the house of Sagittarius as it opens your mind to higher ideals and larger opportunities.

Often referred to as a "guardian angel," Jupiter's house shows an area of life where you have more luck than most. However, it is important not to take Jupiter's blessing for granted and overexpand, overindulge or overreact to outside circumstances. Yes, you are "guarded" here. You are protected. Count your blessings and enjoy.

Saturn

Just as Saturn's rings draw boundaries around the planet, Saturn operates in the birth chart to draw limits around activity. Saturn is the law enforcer, drawing boundaries around the activities of its house until you learn to appreciate all things within those limits. And yet, this planet is a blessing in disguise. Bringing responsibility, reality and sometimes frustration to be confronted and overcome, Saturn promises rewards for jobs well done.

Saturn rules Capricorn. To gain the prestige and recognition desired in the experiences ruled by Capricorn's house, you must earn it through work, perseverance and self-discipline with Saturn. Capricorn shows where you want respect, while Saturn's house describes where that respect must be earned. In the area of your life ruled by Saturn's house, there are no fringes, but basic realities that must be confronted and accepted if life is to be meaningful in a productive sense. Here, you must earn whatever you desire. Seldom are things offered with no strings attached. Responsibility is, without a doubt, the message of this potent planet.

While the Moon represents the maternal instincts and shows how (sign) and where (house) they have been shaped by past experiences with your mother, Saturn's house shows an area of life strongly influenced (positively or negatively) by the father. Its sign describes a quality which has been inherited or developed as a result of paternal involvement. Saturn's house shows where you need to develop confidence in your own ability to function as an authority.

In Capricorn you need limits; you need to know where your social territory begins and ends. Saturn helps you, through the experiences of its house, to establish that territory, to define and protect it once established. While it is true that what comes through Saturn is not easily acquired, it is equally true that the results of using its energy productively in dealing with responsibility and living in reality brings rewards which are often more gratifying than what comes easily. Through Saturn's experiences you learn to appreciate what you have earned because you have acquired it through your own labors of love.

Saturn brings things into a very clear focus. You are required to deal with the experiences of its house realistically. By attempting to escape the lessons it brings, you find yourself more deeply entangled in the learning experience. Saturn keeps you rooted and gives you structure. Saturn offers respect, recognition and success, but only if it's earned.

Uranus

While Saturn sets limits, it is the function of Uranus to break out of limiting conditions and attitudes in order to be awakened to your higher intelligence and capabilities. While Aquarius, the sign ruled by Uranus, describes where (house) you need to break out of rigid patterning, Uranus provides the energy and experiences by which this breaking away takes place. Aquarius shows where you need to realize that you are more than what you were taught to be. You are, in fact, capable of greater accomplishments than the skills you were taught reveal. Awareness of these greater life possibilities is aroused as a result of the awakening experiences (sometimes the abrupt changes) which take place in the house of Uranus. Uranus tears down obsolete structures. It represents your urge to rebel against whatever social obstacles stand in the way of your growth and future development.

As will be discussed in a later chapter, all planets operate in sequential order, according to their orbital distance from the earth. In other words, the Uranus energy cannot operate creatively until limits have been first established and recognized through Saturn's function. Once you have learned to live productively within the "system," you are qualified to see where changes are needed. Then you can use your Uranus-energy to break down rigidity or structures that have been proven to be obsolete. Until Saturn has defined, in specific terms, what is expected by society, Uranus cannot function creatively. If Saturn is left undeveloped, Uranus will show, by house, where your rebellious energy can get you into trouble rather than freeing you from self-imposed or social limitations.

Uranus, by house, shows where life will be full of changes as it challenges you continually to progress, to look ahead, to use your originality, creative insights and intuition to make your mental images realities. You may need to rebel. You may seem to be, in others' eyes, somewhat eccentric in your attitudes. Your chart encourages the development of your individuality here as long as you "know" what you're doing. In essence, look to Uranus' house to find where life won't be dull; where life is challenging you to develop beyond social expectations and where you need to be open to future possibilities even if your ideas do not conform to the status quo.

Neptune

Neptune's function has been likened to an umbilical cord connecting man with his Creator, a channel through which we are fed inspiration and spiritual substance. On the other hand, it acts as a dissolvent, dissolving material or physical obstacles which limit spiritual and inspirational flow. Neptune rules those things which are formless, teaching you to develop faith in what is unknown, to realize the value of that which has no physical form or scientific formula. Due to its rulership over formlessness, Neptune has been associated with confusion and with fogging our perspective of reality. Some use its energy to escape from reality rather than to tune into what is larger than real. It is important to realize, however, that Neptune is not the deceiver—it is our application of its energy that often leads us astray.

In the majority of charts, Neptune indicates where there are "blind spots," describing where you must look beyond what is obvious in a physical sense to find a larger meaning. Due to its reign over all that is illusive, nebulous and invisible, it is easy to be deluded by our own Neptunian energy. At the most positive level, Neptune enables you to develop true psychic abilities, to make contact with a "spiritual guide," whether you find that guide as another entity separate from yourself, or as contact with a universal mind, or as an attunement with your own inner, invisible soul. From a negative level Neptune represents fear of the formless, superstition and confusion which encourages disillusionment and deception when you refuse to look at the reality behind your ideals. There is a fine line between inspiration and delusion. As Neptune draws no boundaries, this invisible line is difficult for all of us to "see."

Neptune rules Pisces. It represents the key needed to reach your Pisces goals. Before true faith and commitment to a larger-than-personal cause can be made, Neptune must first function to dissolve overly rigid or selfish attitudes. Once done, its energy enables you to connect your psyche with the collective unconscious of humanity. What Pisces needs in terms of commitment, wholeness and dedication, Neptune helps us reach out to find. In this search you will find where (house) and how (sign) you could be fooling yourself, avoiding dealing with issues which must be handled realistically before your ideals can be reached.

Pluto

Pluto has been recently associated with cultural and social evolution and change. It stays in one sign anywhere from 12 to 30 years and makes a statement, by sign, concerning changes that are occurring around the globe. Its orbit is erratic, symbolizing the speed at which society has gone through major changes throughout history. At this time, Pluto is moving at its fastest pace. Few can argue that our world is changing rapidly.

Pluto's placement in your chart describes where and how you are playing a part in these social changes as well as how you are consciously or unconsciously contributing to them and being affected by them. Its function is one of regeneration. As ruler of Scorpio, Pluto challenges you to look deeply into your subconscious and to weed out or regenerate whatever is found which has proven undesirable. Due to social changes, you are challenged to alter some of your attitudes and expectations concerning the matters ruled by Pluto's house. The general condition of society itself will play a strong part in what you will experience here. This does not imply that you have no control over the department of life described by Pluto's house, but it does suggest a need for change, and it promises that change will be experienced.

While Scorpio shows where regeneration is needed and where you unconsciously seek intense involvements which create change, Pluto describes, by house, where the regeneration actually takes place. Repressions in Scorpio's house surface through your Pluto activities. The revelations resulting from experiences attracted via Pluto make conscious your need to make personal changes along with your need to play a part in world growth. Pluto has been described as the "part of God that became trapped in His own creation." It represents your ability not just to find and be spiritually fed by this God (such as is Neptune's role), but your ultimate power to become one with this higher force . . . something only few mortals have actually experienced. In essence it represents a "higher power" attempting to work through each of us and it will do so consciously or unconsciously, be it through positive or seemingly negative or destructive acts.

Pluto lets you know when you have gone beyond not only society's boundaries, but also God's. Seldom are people aware of Pluto's deeper functioning in their lives, but once it has been experienced, there is little doubt that a greater force is working through each of us. Our lesson with Pluto is to use this power as a contribution to humanity rather than as a control over it.

PLANETS

Personal — SUN: INDIVIDUALITY, EGO; Our conscious life purpose

Social — door between self & society

Unconscious — door between conscious & unconscious

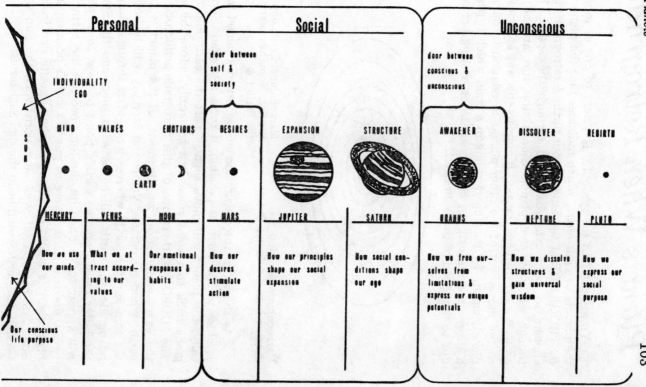

Personal	MERCURY	MIND	How we use our minds
Personal	VENUS	VALUES	What we attract according to our values
Personal	MOON (EARTH)	EMOTIONS	Our emotional responses & habits
Social	MARS	DESIRES	How our desires stimulate action
Social	JUPITER	EXPANSION	How our principles shape our social expansion
Social	SATURN	STRUCTURE	How social conditions shape our ego
Unconscious	URANUS	AWAKENER	How we free ourselves from limitations & express our unique potentials
Unconscious	NEPTUNE	DISSOLVER	How we dissolve structures & gain universal wisdom
Unconscious	PLUTO	REBIRTH	How we express our social purpose

Planets When Retrograde

You might find the symbol (℞) next to one or more of the planets in your chart, which indicates that the planet was RETROGRADE at the time of your birth. A retrograde planet appears to be moving backward through the zodiac. Even though we know that planets cannot stop, turn around, and go backward through the sky, it appears this way at times due to the movement of the other planets in relation to our own planet, earth. To passengers riding in a train which is passing a slower moving car, the car appears to be moving backward due to the speed of the train itself.

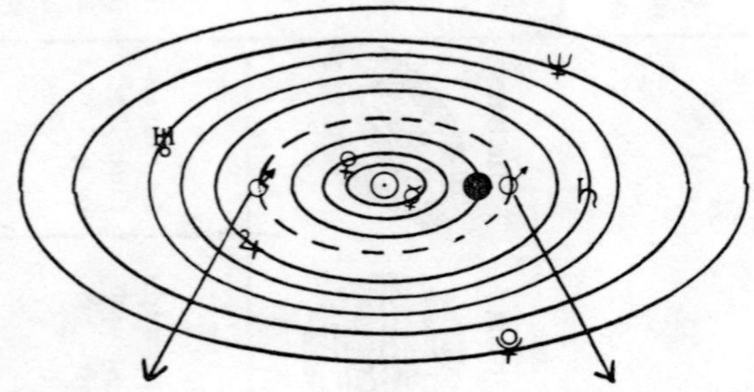

Mars conjunct Sun. Note the distance from the Earth (●).

Mars conjunct Earth, opposite the Sun. Note the closeness to the Earth (●).

As shown in the illustration above, when a planet moves as close to the earth as possible, it turns retrograde. Technically, the planet will move slightly past the earth and retrograde back to a point where it is zodiacally before the earth. The MIDPOINT, therefore, of this retrograde period occurs at the exact conjunction, or alignment, of the planet with the earth. When retrograde, Venus and Mercury will be between the Sun and the earth, whereas when Mars through Pluto are retrograde, the earth will be between them and the Sun. In the latter case, from the earth's point of view, these planets will appear to be opposite the Sun, because the earth is between the two. If we were to put the earth's position in the birth chart it would be placed in the opposite sign from the Sun. For example, if you were born when the Sun was in Gemini, the earth would be in the sign Sagittarius.

Each planet remains retrograde for a different length of time depending on its orbital cycle. At the midpoint of its retrograde period it will be as close to the earth as possible, implying that the purpose, or function, of the retrograde planet is TO COME HOME to be personally confronted and worked with. While a complete text could be written on the retrograde planets, you will find that the basic message of a planet in this condition involves introspection. You are challenged to investigate the importance of each retrograde planet's function in your life and to take full responsibility for its expression, rather than allowing social factors to influence you too strongly. Because the functioning of a retrograde planet is so subjective, you may find it difficult to express through objective avenues. You are challenged to develop that part of yourself ON YOUR OWN. All external factors associated with the retrograde planet must be internalized and made personal before they operate productively.

In most cases, early relationships have caused one to suppress the natural expression of the retrograde planets. Therefore, these functions must be rebuilt before finding a satisfactory mode for expressing the energy they represent. Due to this restructuring process the functions represented by these planets take on a uniqueness in their final expression once they have been internally developed. In general, Mercury through Mars, when retrograde, show the rebuilding of personality. Jupiter and Saturn, when retrograde, involve the rebuilding of social attitudes and conditioning. Retrograde Uranus, Neptune or Pluto transform the unconscious and seem, therefore, less obvious from a personal point of view. (See illustration on page 103 for information on the division of personal, social and unconscious or collective planets.)

There is a similarity between the interpretation of retrograde planets and intercepted signs. However it should be noted that intercepted signs deal with environmental limitations rather than the personal urges or energies needing redirection which are shown by retrograde planets. Too often astrologers fail to make this distinction.

When planets are retrograde, they appear to be moving backward through the signs. In a similar manner, we can find clues to the meaning of retrograde planets by looking at the signs of their rulership in reverse of their usual order. For example . . .

MERCURY when DIRECT: First you gather information from a variety of sources and learn through communication with others (Gemini). Then, you find a practical avenue through which to apply that information, filing what is meaningful and eliminating what is superficial (Virgo). When Mercury is RETROGRADE, the mental function is internalized. You must first analyze information and relate it to your own experiences, perfecting your understanding (Virgo), before successful communication skills are developed (Gemini).

VENUS when DIRECT: First you develop personal values and appreciation for your own worth as an individual, learning to love yourself (Taurus) so that you have something valuable to contribute to a relationship that involves love for another (Libra). When Venus is RETROGRADE, your values must be internalized, which, at first, makes them hard to express. It is difficult to see yourself as valuable (Taurus) until you have developed true concern for others and have received the feedback relationships provide (Libra).

MARS when DIRECT: First, you learn to initiate activity independently, moving out to get what you desire (Aries). Then, identification with personal desire must be eliminated in order to work as a unit with another (Scorpio). When Mars is RETROGRADE, the desire energy is, at first, suppressed. Personal feelings of inadequacy or fear emerge until deep involvements with something outside yourself (Scorpio) release desire and motivation, and a personal sense of identity is formed (Aries).

JUPITER when DIRECT: First, you need to expand your life and broaden your horizons through larger, social experiences (Sagittarius). This leads to the formation of spiritual commitments and a recognition of your oneness with, and responsibilities to, mankind (Pisces). When Jupiter is RETROGRADE, the social urge is internalized, and conditioned beliefs are inwardly changed. Lessons in faith and commitment to your inner beliefs (Pisces) enable you to re-shape conditioned social principles and expectations (Sagittarius).

SATURN when DIRECT: First, you need to define your place in the social structure. Here, you build boundaries around experiences in order to establish yourself in the world around you (Capricorn). Then, your social position and the acceptance of social responsibilities lead you into group activities through which you develop humanitarian concepts and are able to break free (Aquarius) from overly rigid patterning. When Saturn is RETROGRADE, an awareness of your place within the group and society is needed (Aquarius) before personal authority is given (Capricorn). You need to restructure your social ego from what it was taught to be (Capricorn) by expressing your inner individuality (Aquarius) before you know where you fit into society.

NOTE: Uranus, Neptune and Pluto do not have dual rulerships. However, in theory, you will find the following relationships applicable.

URANUS when DIRECT: The unconscious urge to break out of socially limited boundaries and to express your true inner uniqueness. You contribute, through your progressive thoughts, to humanitarian causes (Aquarius) and thereby build a more satisfying social identity than that provided by early authoritarian figures (Capricorn). When Uranus is RETROGRADE, you need to transform rebellious urges (Aquarius) through discipline (Capricorn). Rather than tearing down old structures (Aquarius), you need to enter the establishment (Capricorn) and transform it from within.

NEPTUNE when DIRECT: Your unconscious urge to dissolve old ego patterns in order to find a sense of oneness with all life. Your ability to transcend the boundaries of the conscious mind and tap into universal truths (Pisces), thereby gaining a wider scope of vision (Sagittarius). When Neptune is RETROGRADE, you need to unveil the mysteries of life by attempting consciously to understand the reality or theory (Sagittarius) behind your ideals (Pisces).

PLUTO when DIRECT: Your unconscious urge to contribute something meaningful to the evolution of our world leads to the destruction of old attitudes (Scorpio) and a re-born identity (Aries). When Pluto is RETROGRADE, your need to live out a larger role in the world is unfulfilled until the personal identity (Aries) is transformed (Scorpio) and you become the person you inwardly want to be.

Signs, Houses & Planets in Application

SUN

Your degree of consciousness. Your sense of purpose or importance in life and potential to exert free will.

SUN SIGN: The nature of your purpose and how you build consciousness. A quality needing development for growth at a personal level.

SUN HOUSE: Where your purpose is developed and the type of experiences which build consciousness and self importance.

LEO HOUSE: Where your purpose seeks release in the outer world. Where you express outwardly your consciousness and will.

5TH HOUSE SIGN: The nature of your purposeful expression once functioning outside yourself. A quality within you that will live on as your legacy.

5TH HOUSE RULING PLANET: How (sign) and where (house) you learn to express your purpose creatively. Where and how your legacy is developed.

MOON

Your emotional responses. Your capacity to nurture and to adapt to change.

MOON SIGN: The way you respond to emotional matters.

MOON HOUSE: Where emotions are stimulated, calling for adaptability.

CANCER HOUSE: Where you need emotional security and a sense of belongingness.

4TH HOUSE SIGN: The nature of your emotional foundations and inner feelings about yourself resulting from early home experiences.

4TH HOUSE RULING PLANET: Where (house) and how (sign) your emotional foundations must be developed and strengthened.

MERCURY

Your capacity to think, use reason and analyze or discriminate.

MERCURY SIGN: How your mind operates. How you communicate, analyze and acquire information.

MERCURY HOUSE: Where knowledge is available and experiences call for logic.

GEMINI HOUSE: Where curiosity urges you to seek new experiences, making connections with others at a mental level.

3RD HOUSE SIGN: How knowledge is used in the environment and the educational facilities available to you within the community.

3RD HOUSE RULING PLANET: Where (house) and how (sign) experiences compel you to operate at a mental level and take advantage of the knowledge available in your environment.

VIRGO HOUSE: Where you find techniques for the practical application of your ideas by using analysis and discrimination.

6TH HOUSE SIGN: The nature of your routine activities and the type of techniques best used in filling personal responsibilities.

6TH HOUSE RULING PLANET: Where (house) and how (sign) you learn to be useful at a daily level.

VENUS

Your capacity to build values, both personal and social. Your ability to attract and to appreciate.

VENUS SIGN: How you attract substances and relationships according to your values. A quality you appreciate in others.

VENUS HOUSE: Where you build personal and relative values. the types of experiences you come to appreciate.

TAURUS HOUSE: Where you apply your values at a practical level to get tangible results.

2ND HOUSE SIGN: The nature of your resources and resourcefulness.

2ND HOUSE RULING PLANET: Where (house) and how (sign) resources are developed and self appreciation must be acquired.

LIBRA HOUSE: Where you need to share your values with others and learn to relate to their needs.

7TH HOUSE SIGN: The nature of your relationships and the type of people you need in order to objectify personal projections and values.

7TH HOUSE RULING PLANET: Where (house) and how (sign) you learn to develop the capacity to relate objectively with others.

MARS

Your ability to "do your own thing." The desire, nature and potential for independent action.

MARS SIGN: How your aggressive urges operate and the nature of your desires.

MARS HOUSE: Experiences which stimulate you to act on desire.

ARIES HOUSE: Where energy is released, providing greater self awareness.

1ST HOUSE SIGN: The outer expression of your identity and the nature of your self image.

1ST HOUSE RULING PLANET: Where (house) and how (sign) the self image is developed.

SCORPIO HOUSE: Where personal desires must be controlled out of respect for others, creating regeneration.

8TH HOUSE SIGN: Attitudes needing regeneration in order to maintain relationships. How you go through life's major changes.

8TH HOUSE RULING PLANET: Where (house) and how (sign) regeneration takes place.

JUPITER

Your capacity to participate with the larger society and expand in social influence. Expansive urges in general.

JUPITER SIGN: The nature of your expansive urges both socially and philosophically.

JUPITER HOUSE: Experiences offering opportunity for expansion.

SAGITTARIUS HOUSE: Where a larger understanding of life develops due to expansive activities.

9TH HOUSE SIGN: The nature of your philosophical principles and the manner with which you approach opportunities for growth.

9TH HOUSE RULING PLANET: Where (house) and how (sign) experiences stimulate expanded learning and a larger understanding of life's principles.

SATURN

Your capacity to define your social role. The urge to operate within structure.

SATURN SIGN: A quality needing structuring and the manner with which you build social awareness.

SATURN HOUSE: Where you must operate within well defined boundaries and concentrate energy.

CAPRICORN HOUSE: Where you face responsibilities and seek social acceptance. Where you need structure.

10TH HOUSE SIGN: The nature of your social reputation and public image.

10TH HOUSE RULING PLANET: Where (house) and how (sign) energy must be applied toward building social foundations. Experiences affecting your reputation.

URANUS

Your ability to express your unconditioned self. The urge to be free from rigid patterning.

URANUS SIGN: The nature of your progressive activities and originality.

URANUS HOUSE: Where you seek freedom from rigid patterning. Where your true genius lies.

AQUARIUS HOUSE: Where you release your unique ideas for the good of the larger whole.

11TH HOUSE SIGN: The nature of your group goals and how you approach the unknown future.

11TH HOUSE RULING PLANET: Where (house) and how (sign) group awareness is developed. Where experiences awaken you to future possibilities.

NEPTUNE

Your urge to dissolve structures and transcend the past.

NEPTUNE SIGN: Social attitudes needing to be dissolved.

NEPTUNE HOUSE: Where you sacrifice personal substances and dissolve selfish desires. Where you are challenged to develop faith in the unknown.

PISCES HOUSE: Where you need to commit yourself to future goals and be of service to others with love.

12TH HOUSE SIGN: The past from which you are escaping and the nature of your social services.

12TH HOUSE RULING PLANET: Where (house) and how (sign) you fill your soul's urge to be a part of the larger whole by contributing to it.

PLUTO

The capacity for regeneration. Your God-potential and ability to plant seed-ideas for future generations.

PLUTO SIGN: The qualities being regenerated by your generation.

PLUTO HOUSE: Where you experience regeneration and where your larger social role lies.

SCORPIO HOUSE: Where you need to control personal desires and unite energies with those of others. Where regeneration is needed.

8TH HOUSE SIGN: Attitudes needing regeneration in order to maintain outer relationships. The way you go through life's changes.

8TH HOUSE RULING PLANET: Where (house) and how (sign) you meet activities which induce regeneration.

ARIES HOUSE: Where a new identity emerges as a result of regeneration.

1ST HOUSE SIGN: The nature of your re-born self image.

1ST HOUSE RULING PLANET: Where (house) and how (sign) you apply your new-found self image toward social regeneration.

Planetary Emphasis in the Signs

It is important to assess the overall "tone" of a chart before going on to the more specific aspects of interpretation. This can be done by evaluating the chart according to the placement of planets in the Qualities and Elements. By making a note of which planets occupy the different Qualities and Elements, you begin to get an overview of the horoscope in terms of behavior patterns and personality.

An abundance of planets located in signs of a particular Quality or Element, along with a significant lack of planets in another Quality or Element will give an important clue to potential overloads or lacks concerning life expression. For example, you might find that your chart has no planets in mutable signs but the fixed Quality is heavily tenanted. This suggests lack of adaptability (few mutable planets) with a tendency to be overly concerned with maintaining that which already exists (emphasis in fixed). No planets in air signs implies difficulty being objective. On the other hand, having an abundance of air planets with few or no planets in the water Element gives a tendency to be overly objective (excessive air) with difficulty expressing at the emotional level (lack of water).

Some books suggest that planets occupying houses numerically corresponding to the Qualities and Elements which are lacking in the chart (cardinal signs/angular houses, mutable signs/Cadent houses, or, air signs/houses of relationships, etc.) compensate for the lack. From charts I have observed, I have found this to be definitely NOT the case. Remember that signs describe attitudes and needs, while houses describe external environmental experiences. When there is a lack of planets in mutable signs, for example, while several planets are in the cadent houses (those corresponding numerically to the mutable signs), greater stress, rather than relief, is experienced. The lack of planets in mutable signs suggests difficulty adapting psychologically to outside circumstances, while a majority of planets in cadent houses promises that you will continually be placed in situations that require adjustment. This can be a real dilemma.

The Chart Tone

As you refer to, and make note of, the planets in your own chart in terms of their placements in the Qualities and Elements, you will probably find an emphasis in one particular Quality and one particular Element. If this is the case, pay attention to those two very important factors. Only ONE sign falls into any one combination of Quality and Element. That sign will describe an important facet of your life expression and therefore is considered to represent the basic "tone" or "signature" of your birth chart. If there is no obvious division or emphasis shown in your chart, the "tone" factor will be of less significance in your chart's interpretation.

Planetary Emphasis in the Houses

It is equally important to consider the basic planetary placements within the house structure, as planets in houses point to areas of focussed activity. As shown outlined below, there are several points to be considered.

Hemispheric Emphasis

When the majority of planets are located in houses BELOW the horizon, energy is focussed on subjective growth, sometimes leading to a lack of objective awareness concerning outside circumstances. The first six houses deal with areas of life involving growth at a personal level. When lacking planets above the horizon (the houses dealing with social growth through external experience), your perspective of life outside yourself could be limited. When the majority of planets are located in houses ABOVE the horizon, energy is focussed on growth through social participation. Having few planets below the horizon, however, can indicate difficulty developing the subjective self.

When the majority of planets are RISING (located in the left side, or ascending, half of the chart), energy is focussed on independent activity. Called a "destiny making" chart pattern, this emphasis gives free reign to exert your will with little outside opposition or dependency. On the other hand, having few planets on the setting half of the chart can indicate lack of awareness concerning the needs of others. When the majority of planets are SETTING (located in the right half, or descending, side of the chart), energy is focussed on relationships. Called a "destiny reaping" chart pattern, this emphasis suggests a strong need for relationships and the feedback, encouragement and stimulation they provide sometimes to the point of dependency. Having few planets on the rising side of the chart can indicate lack of self awareness or personal initiative.

Stelliums

Stelliums are groupings of four or more planets in one house of the chart. This condition suggests intense energy being expressed within the experiences of the house containing the grouping, which can result in frustration—an overload of energy which seems to ignite the experiences ruled by the house. It is important to make a conscious effort to keep these planets (or personality functions) working harmoniously together, as the degree of integration and mutual cooperation in handling the experiences of the house will determine the fulfillment found in the areas of life, or houses, RULED by the planets in the stellium.

For example, in the following chart there is a stellium in the 6th house consisting of Saturn, Uranus, Mercury and Venus. This suggests a strong need to establish an efficient routine for handling daily responsibilities involving work and health maintenance (6th house). This stellium shows the need

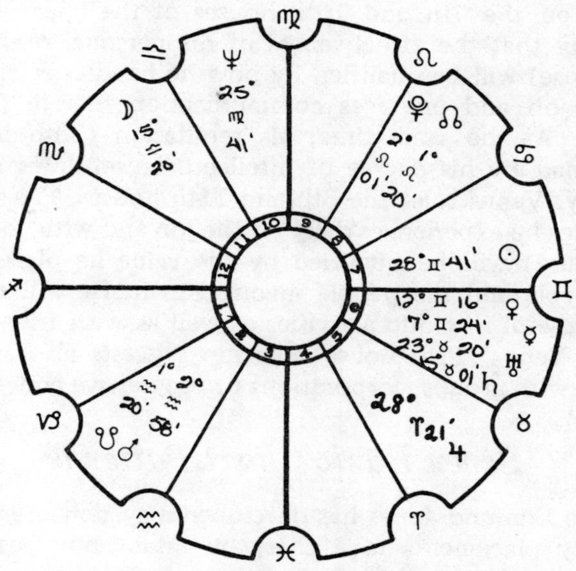

Ed. Note: The above chart has been invented to provide examples of specific factors.

to establish a routine which provides opportunity for unique, original self expression (Uranus), responsibility, structure and recognition (Saturn), intellectual stimulation and communication (Mercury) and diplomatic, valuable, social exchange (Venus). By looking to the houses RULED by these 6th house planets you will find just how important this stellium is in determining the degree of fulfillment in the departments of life described by their houses.

The degree to which this individual establishes a responsible routine which allows the regular expression of each planet qualifies the happiness he will experience in the houses they RULE. As Saturn rules the 2nd house, his self worth (2nd house) is qualified by his ability to handle responsibility in an organized fashion at a daily level (6th house). On the other hand, Uranus rules the 3rd house, so the uniqueness and originality of his ideas are qualified by the opportunities he finds to express them as a part of his daily routine to see how they actually work. Mercury rules both Gemini and Virgo, located on the 7th and 10th houses of the chart. Here we could say that the effectiveness of his personal relationships (7th house) will be qualified by how he handles relationships on the job and practices communication therein (Mercury in 6th). At the same time, his reputation (10th house) is determined by his degree of intellectual usefulness and productivity. Venus rules the 6th and 11th houses. The successes or failures he experiences daily on the job and with co-workers (6th house) will be qualified by the value he places on his routine role and the people involved in it. He will also need to feel useful in group activities as well as with friends (11th house). Venus' 11th house rulership suggests also an ability to work with groups, corporations or progressive concepts.

Seven Basic Chart Patterns

Marc Edmund Jones has developed a system of evaluating planetary placements in a chart by establishing seven basic chart types. You will find extensive information on this subject in his book, *A Guide to Horoscope Interpretation.* Below, however, you will find brief descriptions which demonstrate each of these seven patterns, and you are encouraged to consider them in your initial chart interpretation. You might find that the planets in your chart do not conform to any of the patterns shown in the samples. If this is the case, your chart may be a combination of two different patterns. If so, consider the interpretation for each pattern as it applies to your life. Realize, however, that statements given for one pattern will be qualified by what is said of another.

BUNDLE: All planets are contained within 1/3 or less of the chart. This individual has the capacity to capitalize on limited resources. Strongly focussed energy narrows interests, providing self sufficiency and concentration but creates inhibitions concerning personal potential.

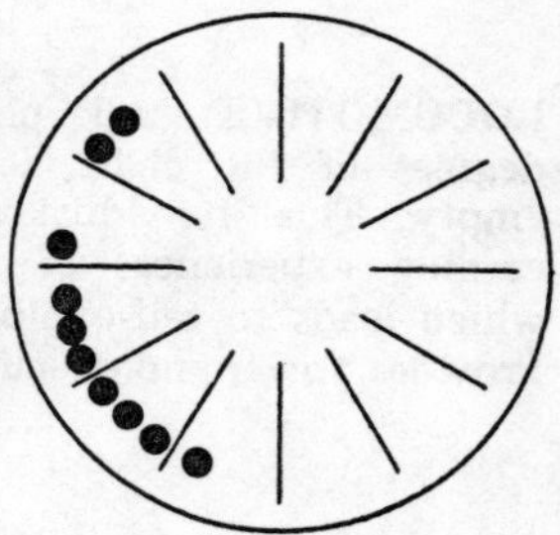

BOWL: All planets are within 180 degrees of the chart but not less than 120 degrees. This individual is self-contained with inner strengths, but feels separate from the fullness of life. Strong focus on either self or society depending on hemispheric emphasis.

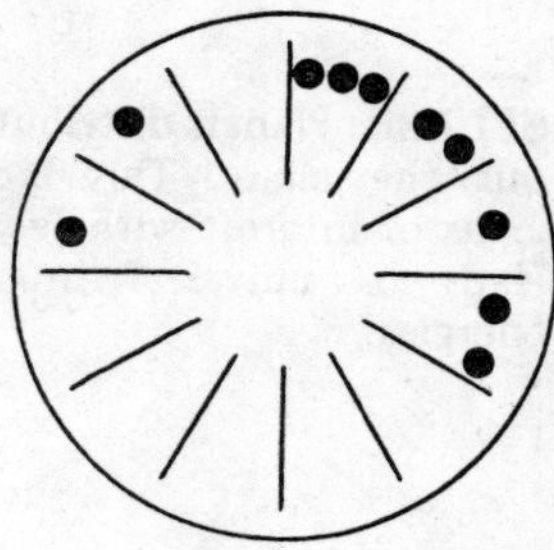

BUCKET: All planets except one are contained within one half (180 degrees) of the chart. This individual is strongly focussed on experiences ruled by the occupied houses. Energy must be funneled through the function of the isolated planet. Until integrated, the isolated planet creates irritation.

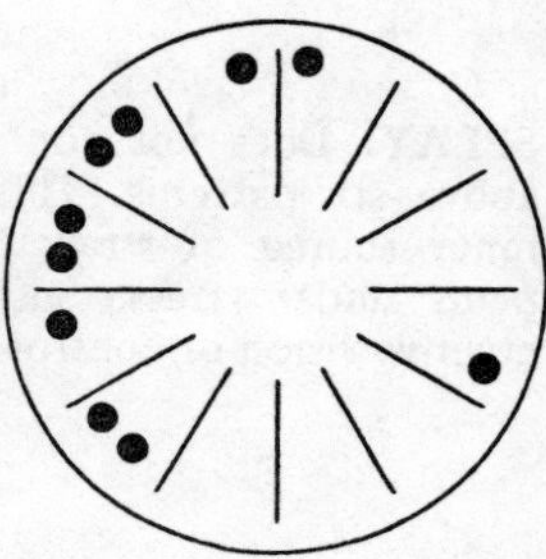

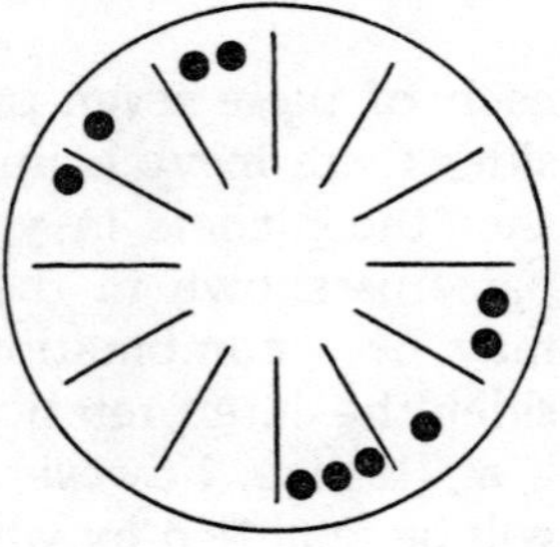

SEE SAW: An obvious grouping of planets opposing another grouping, creating a see-saw picture. This individual develops objectivity or imbalances according to the ability to balance opposing views. Awareness of constant opposition, alternatives or tension in life.

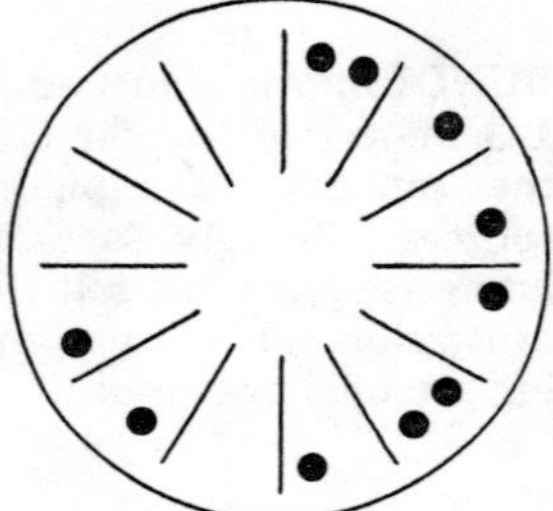

LOCOMOTIVE: All planets within 240 degrees of the chart, leaving 120 or 1/3 empty. This individual senses a lack concerning experiences of the empty houses which leads to self-exploration and growth. Provides power and executive ability.

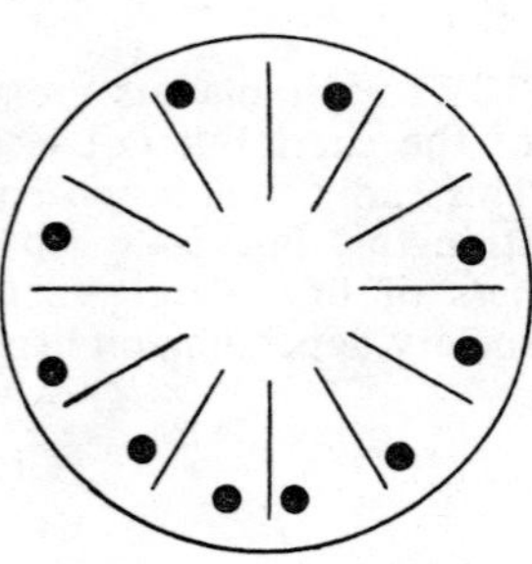

SPLASH: Planets distributed equally throughout the chart. This individual has broad areas of interest with few inhibitions. Either leads to universal interests or scattered energies.

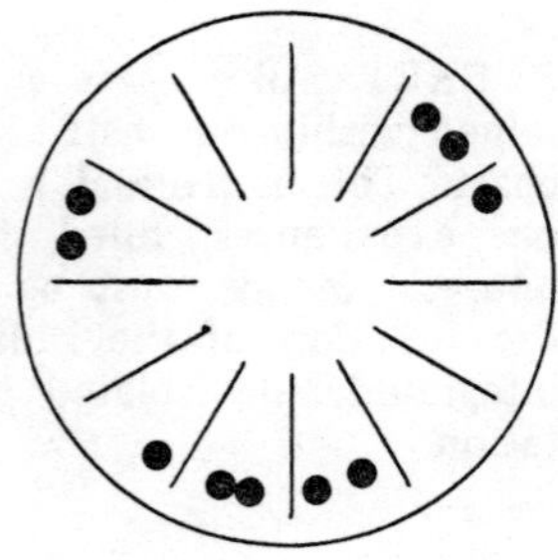

SPLAY: Does not conform to any of the above six patterns. This individual has an inner source of strength on which to depend under stress. Sustaining energy and creative vision or control over others.

More on the Planets

Each planet moves through the signs at a different rate of speed according to its distance from the earth. As the Moon is not actually a planet, but a satellite of the earth, its orbit is much faster than those of the planets. The Moon completes its cycle around the zodiac in a little less than 28 days. Pluto, on the other hand, because of its great distance from the earth, is the slowest moving of all planets in terms of its zodiacal cycle. There are periods, due to Pluto's eccentric orbit, when it enters the orbit of Neptune. In general terms, however, Pluto is considered to be beyond Neptune due to the total time it takes to make one full orbit around the zodiac. Here you will find a list of planetary speeds. This order should be memorized for future application when you begin working with aspects.

Planetary Speed

PLANET	GEOCENTRIC CYCLE
Moon	28 days
Mercury	approx. 1 year.
Venus	approx. 1 year.
Sun	approx. 1 year.
Mars	2 years.
Jupiter	12 years.
Saturn	28 years.
Uranus	84 years.
Neptune	165 years.
Pluto	248 years.

A rule to remember, especially when working with the aspects discussed in the next chapter, is that the slower the planet moves, the more powerful its ultimate influence. Slower planets SHAPE the expression of all those with a faster orbit. For example, the Moon deals with instinctual, emotional responses. These feelings, or emotions, are continually shaped by outer circumstances. Mercury, as it moves more slowly than the Moon through the signs, shapes emotional responses by providing logic and reason. It provides the capacity to rationalize your responses, to think about them before acting on them. Venus, on the other hand, moves more slowly than Mercury. It provides a value system, enabling you to evaluate the significance of your thoughts (Mercury) and feelings (Moon). The Sun gives purpose to your feelings, your thoughts and values. It provides consciousness and direction required to use your Mars energy which follows to encourage you to move outside yourself and take action on what you consider valuable or desirable. Jupiter, next in orbit, encourages you to expand your realm of influence and social activities, to participate in larger social experiences. Saturn comes next to establish limits and regulations around your social involvements. Saturn is the law enforcer. Uranus, once Saturn has fulfilled its purpose, encourages you to extend beyond the "norm," to develop beyond society's expectations of you. Then Neptune illumines you to a higher goal, dissolving ego-attachments while giving awareness of universal principles. Pluto, last in order, is the final boundary-marker. It is the "God within" which ultimately shapes all that you do.

The Aspects

You have probably noticed through your own observations that certain sign combinations operate more compatibly together than others. In your own life, for example, you may find yourself drawn to people of one sign while irritated by people of another. However, such compatibility and conflict factors are evident within the individual as well as in relationships. These inner conflicts and talents can be seen when looking to the *ASPECTS* in the individual chart. Some planets in your chart may occupy signs that are essentially compatible with each other, while other planets will occupy signs that arouse irritation and conflict. Signs of the same Element tend to complement while signs of the same Quality create irritation. Generally speaking, signs of the same gender function together with ease.

Aspects are found by determining the angular relationship between each planet to all others in the chart. There are six major aspects that should be considered when interpreting each horoscope. These aspects include:

Aspect	Glyph	Degrees Between Planets	Orb of Aspect
Conjunction	☌	0	8 degrees
Sextile	✱	60	6 degrees
Square	□	90	8 degrees
Trine	△	120	8 degrees
Quincunx or Inconjunct	⚻	150	4 degrees
Opposition	☍	180	8 degrees

It is not the purpose of this book to provide descriptions of each possible aspect between each individual planet, but rather to help YOU to form your own conclusions regarding what each aspect infers. To view aspects as a singular point of a chart's interpretation can limit your ability to recognize other synthesizing factors.

Some important rules to consider when looking at aspects are:

1. The slower moving planet is ultimately SHAPING and influencing the expression of the faster planets.

2. The conditions described by the house(s) RULED by the faster moving planet are influenced by the slower planet's aspect.

3. The conditions described by the house(s) CONTAINING the aspecting planets are influenced by the aspect.

Examples will be provided to help you understand the basic approach which should be taken when interpreting aspects. Refer to the chart on the following page when reading the examples given.

THE CONJUNCTION

Conjunctions (☌) occur when two or more planets are located within an 8 degree space. In most cases planets in conjunction occupy the same sign, although this aspect can occur when one planet is near the end of a sign while another is placed in the early degrees of the following sign. An important factor to remember when locating conjunctions is that the planets must be within an 8 degree orb of a 360 degree circle. (Astrologers vary on orb allowance for aspects. The orbs listed here are those most commonly used, but you may want to experiment with them after your initial introduction to aspects.)

When a conjunction occurs in a natal chart both planets are challenged to work TOGETHER as a team. This aspect can create ease or tension depending on the nature of the planets involved. For example, note the conjunction between Saturn and Venus in the sample chart. This particular configuration is considered, by most, to be a difficult one due to the contrast of the two planetary functions. Saturn's urge is to restrict until a structured definition of importance has been made. Venus, on the other hand, describes love instincts, and the potential to attract what is desirable. The Venus function seems squelched or inhibited by Saturn's responsibilities. The NEED described by this particular combination involves putting into a structured perspective one's sense of worth,

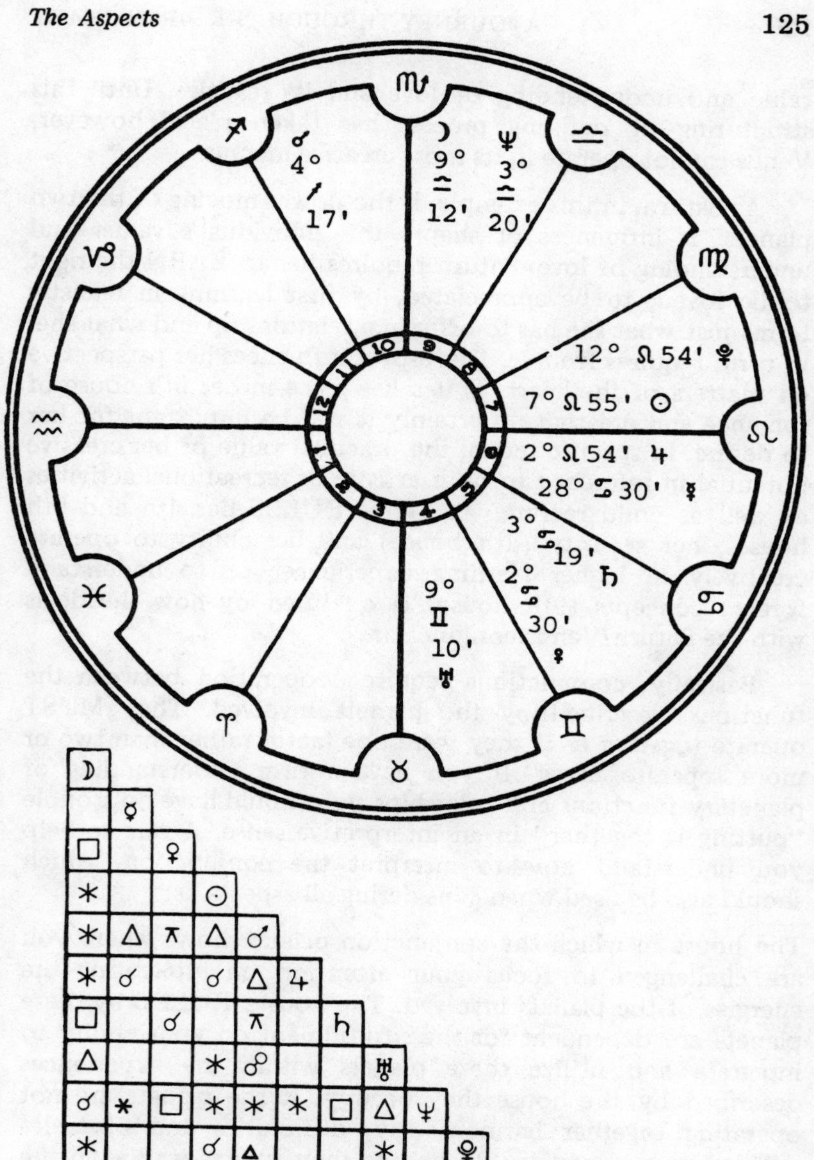

☽									
	☿								
□		♀							
✱			☉						
✱	△	⊼	△	♂					
✱	☌		☌	△	♃				
□		☌		⊼		♄			
△			✱	☍			♅		
☌	✱	□	✱	✱	✱	□	△	♆	
✱			☌	▲			✱		♇

Ed. Note: The above chart has been invented to provide examples of specific factors.

value and understanding of love and its realities. Until this structuring or defining process has taken place, however, Venus cannot operate in its most creative manner.

As Saturn, in this example, is the slower moving of the two planets, it influences or shapes this individual's values and understanding of love. Saturn requires her to EARN the right to be loved, to be appreciated, by first learning in realistic terms just what she has to offer in a relationship and what she, in turn, requires from it. This aspect influences her perspective on matters of the heart, as it takes place in her 5th house of romance and creativity. Certainly it will be important for her to define, in specific terms, the practical value of her creative potential in reference to both artistic or recreational activities as well as child rearing. As Venus RULES her 4th and 9th houses, her security (4th house) and her ability to operate creatively in higher learning experiences or to understand foreign concepts (9th house) is qualified by how she deals with the Saturn/Venus conjunction.

Basically, conjunctions require cooperation between the functions described by the planets involved. They MUST operate together as if they were one factor rather than two or more separate urges. If you have a firm understanding of planetary functions and rulerships you should have no trouble "putting it together" in an interpretive sense. A rule to help you understand how to interpret the conjunction, which should also be used when considering all aspects, is:

The house in which the conjunction occurs shows where you are challenged to focus your attention on integrating the energies of the planets involved. The houses RULED by these planets are dependent for their fulfillment on your ability to integrate and utilize these planets within the experiences described by the house they occupy. If the planets are not operating together harmoniously, difficulties and obstacles will be experienced in the houses they rule as well as in the house they occupy.

THE SEXTILE

Any two or more planets residing within a 6 degree orb of a 60 degree angle are in a sextile (*) aspect. To locate all aspects, other than the conjunction, it is important to realize that there are 30 degrees in each sign (not necessarily in each house). Therefore, in general terms, Gemini is in a sextile relationship with Aries. Cancer, on the other hand, is in a 60 degree relationship with Taurus and so on around the wheel. In essence, planets that are two signs apart, regardless of their house arrangement, and within a 6 degree orb of being in the same degree, are SEXTILE. Because planets in sextile share the same gender, this aspect is considered to be compatible and relatively easy. The planets involved share similar approaches to life situations, either being assertive (masculine) or receptive (feminine) in their outlook and expression. When planets are within the required orb of a sextile aspect they assist each other in functioning.

In the case of a sextile, the slower moving planet, through the experiences it encounters or promotes in its house, encourages and provides opportunity for you to utilize the function of the faster planet within the framework of its experience. For example, in the sample chart you will find a sextile between Mars in Sagittarius and the Moon in Libra. They are within 6 degrees of the exact 60 degree angle. In this case the individual will find that as she initiates new activities and utilizes her personal energies within her career (Mars in 10th house) she finds opportunity to share her feelings (Moon) concerning her beliefs and cultural principles (9th house). This aspect, from a more traditional point of view, also invites travel (9th house) or other types of foreign affairs in association with her career (10th house).

The sextile promises that activities resulting from the energies being expressed by the slower planet will provide opportunity to use the energies of the faster planet, BUT you must reach out to meet these opportunities or they will pass by. Effort is required here, but only in the sense that you must reach out for what is available rather than waiting idly for the opportunity to come to you.

Due to the orb allowance of 6 degrees, you might find sextiles between two planets which are not of the same gender. Pay particular attention when recording your aspects so that these configurations are not overlooked. For example, in the sample chart, Mercury in a late degree of Cancer is sextile to Neptune at 3 degrees of Libra. Notice that Mercury is about to enter Leo. As each sign contains 30 degrees, Mercury is 65 degrees from Neptune. This is within the required 6 degree orb of the 60 degree angle. Other sextile aspects located in the sample chart are shown in the aspectarian provided below the chart.

THE SQUARE

Any two planets within an 8 degree orb of a 90 degree angle are in square aspect (□). In most cases these planets occupy signs of the same Quality but of a different Element. One planet will be in a masculine sign while the other occupies a feminine sign. While planets in signs of the same Element function together harmoniously due to the temperamental similarities, planets in signs of the same Quality function under stress. When planets occupy different signs in a particular Quality, they are, in essence, working against each other. For example, Libra, when seen in relation to nature's unfoldment, suggests a harvest is ready to be reaped. Capricorn, on the other hand, suggests that crops have already returned to the earth. Symbolically, these two signs demonstrate a conflict of purpose. Both are cardinal, but Libra is an air sign, while Capricorn is in the earth element. When planets are within an 8 degree orb of an exact 90 degree angle, stress requiring adjustment becomes intense in the individual life.

Before going on to discuss the square in detail, consider the general conflicts posed by signs in each quality:

CARDINAL CONFLICT

ARIES . . . Can you do your own thing without . . .
CANCER . . . risking your security, while . . .

LIBRA . . . working harmoniously with others and . . .
CAPRICORN . . . still remain in authority?

FIXED CONFLICT

TAURUS . . . Can you operate at a practical level without . . .
LEO . . . overextending your self-importance while . . .
SCORPIO . . . experiencing ego regeneration through intense involvements and still . . .
AQUARIUS . . . be a unique, independent individual?

MUTABLE CONFLICT

GEMINI . . . Can you learn from a variety of experiences while . . .
VIRGO . . . using all knowledge productively and still . . .
SAGITTARIUS . . . understand the larger point of view without . . .
PISCES . . . losing yourself in the imaginative realms?

As with all aspects, when interpreting squares, the slower planet is the challenging or shaping factor. The experiences it creates or attracts through its house cause tension in the area of life described by the house containing the faster planet. Consider the slower planet to represent growth experiences which challenge old patterns of expression concerning the way you have been using the energy of the faster planet.

For example, in the sample chart note the square between Neptune in the 9th house and the Venus/Saturn conjunction in the 5th. As Neptune is the slower planet, it describes the new directives necessary in life. The challenge of Neptune is to dissolve old belief systems and look beyond society's ideas of religion or theory (9th house) in order to find something meaningful in which to believe. In the process of dissolving old beliefs this individual will confront a crisis (square) involving past attitudes about romance, self-importance and the use of her creative energy (5th house). Conditioned ideas (Saturn) about all 5th house matters (romance, child rearing, creativity and the ability to attract others into her life with Venus) are dissolved by the Neptunian energy. As the aspect is a square, a lesson will be learned through a crisis of some kind. When looking at the aspect in terms of the cardinal conflict, the challenge requires her to be aware of others' needs and expectations (Libra) rather than clinging to her own emotional attachments for support (Cancer).

In essence, the square requires CHANGE. Until changes have been made concerning the functioning of the faster planet, frustration and obstacles will be confronted. In the example given above, she could easily fool herself or be fooled by others when it comes to romantic attractions. This aspect encourages her to look beyond the immediate (Neptune in 9th house) and to have faith in a higher power so that unfortunate 5th house experiences can be avoided.

While they do involve conflict, squares do not indicate a life long problem unless you don't learn from the lessons they present. This aspect is basically "provoking." Squares challenge you to break out of old patterns which the chart suggests have been outgrown. The degree to which conflicts presented by squares are worked through will determine the level of fulfillment gained within the experiences RULED by the aspecting planets. In other words, not only are the houses containing planets in square challenged, but the conditions shown by the houses they rule are equally stressed. Squares are not "bad" or "malefic" in nature as many older astrological literature suggests. They are progressive, stimulating excitement and growth. Growth, however, is seldom easy. Therefore, the square is considered to be a challenging and, yes, sometimes quite a difficult aspect.

SQUARES in CARDINAL signs are strong, as the cardinal Quality is initiating and active by nature. Therefore, cardinal squares ignite action, requiring you to promote change rather than wait for outside circumstances to provoke the inevitable.

SQUARES in FIXED signs are more difficult, as the fixed Quality tends toward stubborness. Fixed signs are geared toward maintaining what already exists, while the square aspect requires change.

SQUARES in MUTABLE signs have less difficulty adjusting to change, as the mutable Quality is adaptable by nature. It is important, however, that you not be so adaptable that results are never experienced or that you scatter your energies too widely.

Always remember to check for "out of sign" aspects. Due to the 8 degree orb allowance, it is possible to find a square taking place between planets that are not in signs of the same Quality. When this happens you will find one planet is about to move out of a sign of a particular Quality and into the Quality the other has just entered. Unfortunately, there are no out-of-sign squares in the sample chart. However, had a planet been anywhere from 26 to 29 degrees of Gemini, it would have been within the required orb of a square to Neptune in the early degrees of Libra.

THE TRINE

Unlike planets in signs of the same Quality, planets occupying signs of the same Element are considered compatible. They function easily together, because they share similar temperaments. For example:

Fire Signs

As all signs in the fire Element are goal oriented in temperament, when you have planets occupying two or more of the fire signs, you find distinct parts of your personality that function harmoniously together as they desire freedom to pursue future goals independently. Planets in ARIES stimulate continued self awareness through progressive, independent activity. Planets in LEO stimulate continued purpose-evolvement through self expression. Planets in SAGITTARIUS stimulate greater understanding of life through extended learning and vast experience. Basically, fire signs support each other, causing no conflict in terms of their cooperative goals.

Earth Signs

Earth signs produce the need for practical living. These signs are concerned with the here and now and provide substances necessary for survival. Planets in TAURUS encourage practical values and determination. Planets in VIRGO encourage practical application of knowledge. Planets in CAPRIcorn encourage practical achievement at a social level.

Again, the needs represented by these signs do not cause conflict but provide mutual support. Therefore, planets sharing this Element function in a mutually supportive manner.

Air Signs

Air signs stimulate the need for mental relationships. Here, in the houses ruled by air signs, you seek out relationships which stimulate your mental processes and encourage objective living. Planets in GEMINI stimulate the need to learn from a variety of experiences and facts. Planets in LIBRA stimulate the need to share ideas with others on a one-to-one basis. Planets in AQUARIUS stimulate the need to develop originality in thinking and to relate intellectually to group needs.

As all air signs are mental in expression and seek people with whom to learn and to communicate there is no stress involved between planets sharing this Element.

Water Signs

Water signs deal with the development of sensitivity and emotion, showing, by house, where the past influences your present experiences and emotional responses. Planets in CANCER stimulate the need to nurture and protect what already exists. Planets in SCORPIO stimulate the need for intense involvements which regenerate past experiences. Planets in PISCES stimulate the need to cultivate faith in the unknown future through the accumulation of collective wisdom gathered from a collective past.

Any two planets within an 8 degree orb of a 120 degree angle are considered to be in a trine (△) aspect. Basically, the trine is a sustaining aspect. These planets function harmoniously together. Supportive, yet non-challenging, trines can also imply laziness unless there are other more challenging aspects to the planets in trine. This aspect is best used to find areas of relief, or ease in functioning. Yet, when looking at a chart of someone who has taken great strides in life, the trine will not be the prominent aspect in the horoscope. The incentive needed to use the creative energy of the trine is gained from the harder aspects (squares, conjunctions and oppositions).

In most cases trines are found when two planets occupy different signs in the same Element and are within the required 8 degree orb. For example, in the sample chart Mars in Sagittarius is trine Jupiter in Leo. Both Sagittarius and Leo share the fire Element, which implies that both planets function on the basis of goals and vision. As Jupiter is the slower moving of the two, it has the shaping effect in this case. The opportunities for ego-expansion (Jupiter in Leo) available in the working environment (the 6th house) provide support and encourage this individual to move ahead independently toward future career or social goals (Mars in Sagittarius in the 10th house).

Trines point to natural talents available to you for use. The energy flowing between planets in trine is creative and requires little, if any, effort. Other trines found in the example chart include both Moon and Neptune trine Uranus. Notice that Mars is in an "out-of-sign" trine with Mercury. Mercury is only 2 degrees from moving into Leo. As Mars is at 4 degrees of Sagittarius, the orb is 6 degrees from being exactly 120 degrees from Mercury.

THE QUINCUNX OR INCONJUNCT

The inconjunct aspect (⚻) is considered by some to be only a minor aspect. Personal observation has led me to believe that its influence deserves more recognition than previously given. It is an aspect of ADJUSTMENT, requiring adaptability due to unforeseen complications or changes. When two planets are in an inconjunct or quincunx aspect, the slower planet, due to the experiences it encounters in its house, causes frustration in fulfilling the goals of the faster moving planet. This does not suggest that the inconjunct aspect is a negative one, but one requiring continual adjustments in life direction. It can be considered exciting once adaptability has been developed. Even though you may not end up where you initially plan to go with your life, the final outcome can be illuminating.

To more fully understand the significance of the inconjunct, visualize yourself getting up and moving about two blocks away. There is a house that you want to see. As you begin moving toward the house, having reached a point where you are almost there, you notice a drop off prohibiting you from going further. This drop off was not visually evident to you until AFTER you began your journey. Your perceptions, due to human visual limitations, could not warn you of the detour you would need to make in order to reach your destination.

As you make your detour you are distracted by something that encourages you to put aside your original idea about going to that particular house. You are invited to look in another direction. Confusing? Yes. Distracting? Certainly. Frustrating? At times. Yet, as you look in the other direction, away from the home you first wanted to see, you find something even more exciting. Maybe it is a new house that you never before noticed that deserves your attention. It is something you never would have found had you not ventured out of the house at all.

This type of experience is what can be expected from the inconjunct aspect. You never really know where you are going until you have moved out after something else. The faster planet, by house and sign, describes the conditions which get you started. The house opposite the faster planet represents the original destination. The slower planet, by house and sign, represents the distraction or the events that necessitate the detour you confront.

The inconjunct is found when two planets are in a 150 degree angle (just one sign short of being opposite from each other). The orb allowance for this aspect is only 4 degrees. In the example chart notice that Mars in Sagittarius is inconjunct, or quincunx, to Venus in the 5th house. This can be interpreted to mean that career involvements (Mars, the slower planet, in the 10th house) cause a need to make an adjustment concerning the direction of this person's creative expression and interests (Venus in the 5th). When she concerns herself with romantic involvements, personal recreation or the creative arts, she will find that her urge to expand her career and social responsibilities (Mars in 10th in Sagittarius) requires her to reevaluate the direction she is moving toward in the more personal areas of her life. What she at first perceives as important is altered due to the encounters met through career. This does not imply that romantic ventures or creative interests will not be successful, but it suggests that her original ideas about these matters will be altered due to 10th house activities.

On the other hand, Saturn is also forming an inconjunct to her 10th house Mars. In this case Saturn is the slower moving planet and therefore represents the personality function that will create the need to make a detour in profession (Mars in 10th). As she DEFINES and develops her sense of self-importance by nurturing her creative projects (Saturn in Cancer in 5th house), she will come to realize that her original professional desires (Mars in 10th) no longer hold the value they originally did. Ideally she will find a way of using her 5th house creative talents as a part of her professional, social role. Even so, each time she gets pulled off the track by either the creative involvement or new professional opportunities, a new adjustment will need to be made.

THE OPPOSITION

The opposition (☍) is an aspect requiring objectivity, awareness and balancing of opposites. An easy aspect to locate in the chart, oppositions involve planets that are 180 degrees apart within an 8 degree orb allowance. This aspect always involves relationships between yourself and others. Therefore, it requires awareness concerning how your actions, motives and/or thoughts are influencing and influenced by external circumstances. The keyphrase for the opposition is, "think before you act," as others will be influenced by your expression.

When considering the opposition, the slower planet, while seeking expression through the activities of its house, puts stress on the functioning of the faster planet, requiring you to be more objective in behavior. Balance is needed. You must develop techniques for harmonizing seemingly opposing factors. The degree of development in one house is reflected through the activities experienced in the opposite.

Oppositions between the 1ST & 7TH HOUSES suggest the need to balance self (1st house) with others (7th house). The quality of your 7th house relationships will be strongly qualified by your degree of self-confidence in meeting life and your level of self-awareness. Until EQUAL concern for self and others has been developed, imbalances in relationships will be evident.

Oppositions between the 2ND & 8TH HOUSES suggest the need to balance personal assets and talents (2nd house) with those of others (8th house) even though personal sacrifices are sometimes necessary. The stability of your life, financially as well as psychologically, is strongly qualified by your ability to share resources and energies with others. Until EQUAL concern for personal and shared assets is developed, imbalances will be evident.

Oppositions between the 3RD & 9TH HOUSES suggest the need to balance personal knowledge acquired through community contact (3rd house) with the knowledge available outside the community (9th house). The stability of your mental life is determined by how you balance knowledge gained from local facilities with that coming to you from larger, social contacts and philosophical environments. In essence, the need here is to find a harmonious way of balancing factual data with abstract theory.

Oppositions between the 4TH & 10TH HOUSES suggest the need to balance your urge for personal security in home and with family (4th house) with your desire for success and recognition at a larger, social level. The challenge here is to keep the home and public life operating together harmoniously rather than sacrificing one at the expense of the other.

Oppositions between the 5TH & 11TH HOUSES suggest the need to balance your urge for self-expression and personal happiness with the need for social contacts and a desire to contribute to group or humanitarian causes. The challenge here involves finding a way to utilize your creative talents in a manner that contributes to the group without sacrificing one for the other. In some cases confusion is experienced between romantic love (5th house) and friendship (11th house). Rather than living for one of these areas only, the challenge is to find harmony between both.

Oppositions between the 6TH & 12TH HOUSES suggest the need to find balance between the routine responsibilities of your daily life (6th house) with your need for privacy and time for spiritual development and self-discovery (12th house). The goal of this opposition involves finding a creative way of fulfilling practical responsibilities without sacrificing spiritual or psychological development, or, on the other hand, without escaping into your own private world to the degree that you avoid handling practical issues in your daily life.

With the opposition there is always the need to balance opposite goals or points of view. Rather than sacrificing one for the other, you need to find a way of harmonizing both poles. Potential imbalances become obvious through the feedback acquired from others. Their reactions can be likened to the "mirror of your soul," illuminating potential problems requiring personal integration. Problems stemming from oppositions are inevitably brought out in relationships. The feedback in relationships enables you to see, objectively, where changes are needed in your life. Therefore, while considered a moderately stressful aspect, all problems associated with the opposition will become obvious to you, enabling you more easily to work through them. The opposition helps you to become more aware or objective about your life and the direction you have chosen to follow.

In the example chart, note the opposition between Uranus and Mars. Not only does this opposition occur in angular houses, but these planets form the outer boundary of the "bowl" chart pattern, indicating that all other planets in the chart must function within the qualifications they describe. Due to these factors, this aspect could be considered the strongest aspect in the chart. Uranus, the slower moving planet, is challenging Mars to operate within its context. As mentioned earlier, the opposition arouses conflicts involving other people. These conflicts make evident the need for greater cooperation and adaptation to the world of others. In this case, we find a potential for argumentative, rebellious (Uranus) action (Mars) which can interfere not only with vocational fulfillment (10th house), but also with family and security matters (4th house). This individual must learn, through the feedback attracted from others (opposition), how to use the combined creative, stimulating, and rather excitable energy provided by this combination of planets in a way that provokes change constructively rather than chaotically. Until greater skills are developed regarding cooperation, the individual will undoubtedly be seen by others as rebellious, overly aggressive and totally unpredictable. Once integrated, however, the energy of Uranus can invoke the power to reform and transform energy.

Planetary Powers

Aspects are not the only way to determine stress and/or supportive factors in the birth chart. The expression of a planet is also influenced by the degree of compatibility between the basic function of the planet and the needs of the sign it occupies. For example, a fiery planet such as Mars finds ease in expression when placed in a fire sign where it is given freedom to "do its own thing." However, Mars, the planet encouraging aggression and self-assertion, in a sign concerned with nurturing and security, such as Cancer, creates a conflict regardless of its aspects to other planets. The use of common sense, along with a comprehensive understanding of the basics of astrology (signs, houses and planets) will enable you to draw your own conclusions concerning the degree of compatibility found by planets in the various signs. However, a *Table of Planetary Powers* is also included here to assist in this evaluation.

At one time astrologers placed a strong emphasis on Planetary Powers (sometimes called Planetary Dignities). Because the original interpretation of these "powers" has become obsolete, many astrologers no longer recognize them as significant. However, valuable information can be gathered by observing them in operation in the birth chart. Unfortunately, the names given to the different "powers" leave something to be desired. No client wants to hear that their Mercury is in "detriment" or that their Mars is in "fall." Such terminology can be frightening.

As shown in the following *Table of Planetary Powers*, there are four categories to be considered. Planets can be located in signs of their *Rulership* (or *Dignity*), *Exaltation*, *Detriment* or *Fall.* In general . . .

PLANETS IN RULERSHIP function naturally with no qualifications placed on their expression.

PLANETS IN EXALTATION function with originality. Any qualifications concerning their outer expression assist rather than detract from these planets.

PLANETS IN DETRIMENT occupy signs opposite from their Rulerships. The creative functioning of these planets requires objectivity and feedback concerning their expression. They show activities which are strongly qualified by external circumstances, operating much like a planet in opposition.

PLANETS IN FALL occupy signs opposite from their Exaltations. Observation has shown that insecurity is often evident in the expression of the personality functions these planets represent.

The guidelines on the following pages should be helpful in understanding the basic implications of planets in the "powers."

PLANETARY POWERS

	RULERSHIP	DETRIMENT	RULERSHIP	DETRIMENT	EXALTATION	FALL
☉	LEO Where self consciousness & purpose are expressed openly & creatively	AQUARIUS Where personal consciousness & ego goals must balance with group goals.			ARIES Where free will & expression of purpose flow thru independent activity.	LIBRA Where self consciousness develops thru relationships leading to insecurity regarding independence.
☽	CANCER Where emotional responses flow freely based on security development.	CAPRICORN Where emotional responses are structured by social conditions & ambitions.			TAURUS Where emotional responses are stablized.	SCORPIO Where emotional responses are intensified, leading to control over others or repression.
☿	GEMINI Where the mind operates freely stimulating a variety of interests.	SAGITTARIUS Where the mind operates in the abstract, confused between fact & theory.	VIRGO Where the mind operates to apply knowledge to practical living.	PISCES Where the logical mind finds confusion between idealism & reality or unconscious factors	AQUARIUS Where the mind is open to new unique areas of learning & humanitarian concepts.	LEO Where the mind is focussed on self growth, unable to perceive facts not applicable to personal life.
♀	TAURUS Where development of personal values provide self esteem.	SCORPIO Where deep relationships test personal values, causing need for regeneration.	LIBRA Where values extend to relationships, leading to balance between self & others.	ARIES Where relationships challenge personal independence, leading to domiňance or loss of identity.	PISCES Where values expand toward universal compassion & beauty beyond the physical.	VIRGO Where discrimination in love results in an overly critical analytical or puritanical value nature.

	RULERSHIP	DETRIMENT	RULERSHIP	DETRIMENT	EXALTATION	FALL
♂	ARIES Where personal desire energy leads to extended self-awareness.	LIBRA Where desire for personal activity is challenged by relationships.	SCORPIO Where desire energy is regenerated & directed toward joint goals.	TAURUS Where personal material or physical desire detract from joint goals.	CAPRICORN Where personal desires are well defined, leading to social achievement.	CANCER Where desire for new activity challenges the emotional security.
♃	SAGITTARIUS Where expansive urge leads to larger consciousness & social participation.	GEMINI Where urge to expand & understand larger viewpoints is limited by the logical mind.	PISCES Where urge to expand manifests spiritually, leading to a sense of oneness with all life.	VIRGO Where urge to expand is thwarted by analytical, disciminating mind.	CANCER Where expansive urges enlarge personal foundations & security boundaries of of the past.	CAPRICORN Where urge to larger understanding is blocked by society or ambitions.
♄	CAPRICORN Where urge to be responsible contributes to social foundations.	CANCER Where emotions are structured creating blocks in expression.	AQUARIUS Where defining principle is applied toward rebuilding, leading to originality.	LEO Where consciousness is structured, leading to ego blocks or crystallization.	LIBRA Where defining principle is applied toward equality & fair play.	ARIES Where structuring of personal identity leads to crystallized concept of "I am" or limits self awareness.
♅	AQUARIUS Where potential to express individuality & uniqueness operates progressively.	LEO Where inner individuality is expressed at a personal level, leading to an ego identification with humanitarian goals			SCORPIO Where regeneration releases inner self and develops humanitarian attitudes.	TAURUS Where fear of losing personal substances or changing old values causes insecurity in expression.

	RULERSHIP	DETRIMENT	RULERSHIP	DETRIMENT	EXALTATION	FALL
♆	PISCES Where urge to dissolve old attitudes leads to awareness of oneness with all life.	VIRGO Where urge to dissolve is analyzed to the degree that the larger goals are lost in the analysis.			CANCER Where urge to dissolve old dependencies leads to the reestablishment of new security boundaries.	CAPRICORN Where urge to dissolve is limited by pre-pre-occupation with structure.
♇	**SCORPIO** Where the urge for regeneration operates with the greatest intensity and power.	**TAURUS** Where the urge for regeneration is challenged by the desire to possess.			(There is yet no consensus regarding the exaltation and fall of Pluto.)	

Decanates

Signs can be interpreted from a more sophisticated point of view by considering the DECANATES. Decanates subdivide each sign into three separate categories, refining the more general interpretation given to them. Remember, each sign contains 30 degrees of space. By dividing these signs further into three 10 degree sections, you are able to give more detailed information on how they operate in your life. The first ten degrees of any sign are in that sign's own decanate. For example, the first ten degrees of Aries are in the Aries/Mars decanate. The 2nd ten degrees, from 10 to 20 degrees of any sign, are considered to be co-ruled by the next sign in the same ELEMENT. For example, a planet between 10 and 20 degrees of Aries is in the Leo/Sun decanate as Leo is the first fire sign following Aries. The 3rd ten degrees, from 20 to 30 degrees of any sign, are co-ruled by the next sign in the same Element. For example, a planet between 20 and 30 degrees of Aries is in the Sagittarius/Jupiter decanate.

Ultimately, what you find when dividing signs into decanates is that each Quality is represented in each sign even though the division itself is based on the Elements. While decanates do not take away from the basic needs and attitudes of the signs, they do provide additional insight into how planets function from a more detailed level. On the following page you will find a chart showing the division of the signs into decanates. Then, an outline is given for their interpretation. I recommend that you consider at least the decante of the Sun, Moon and Ascendant.

A Guide for Using Decanates

Aries

0 to 10 degrees (Aries/Mars). Pure instinctive action leads to self-awareness, but often impulsive. Emphasizes the Cardinal energy.

10 to 20 degrees (Leo/Sun). Provides sustaining power to the Aries impulsiveness, but often willful. Emphasizes the Fixed energy.

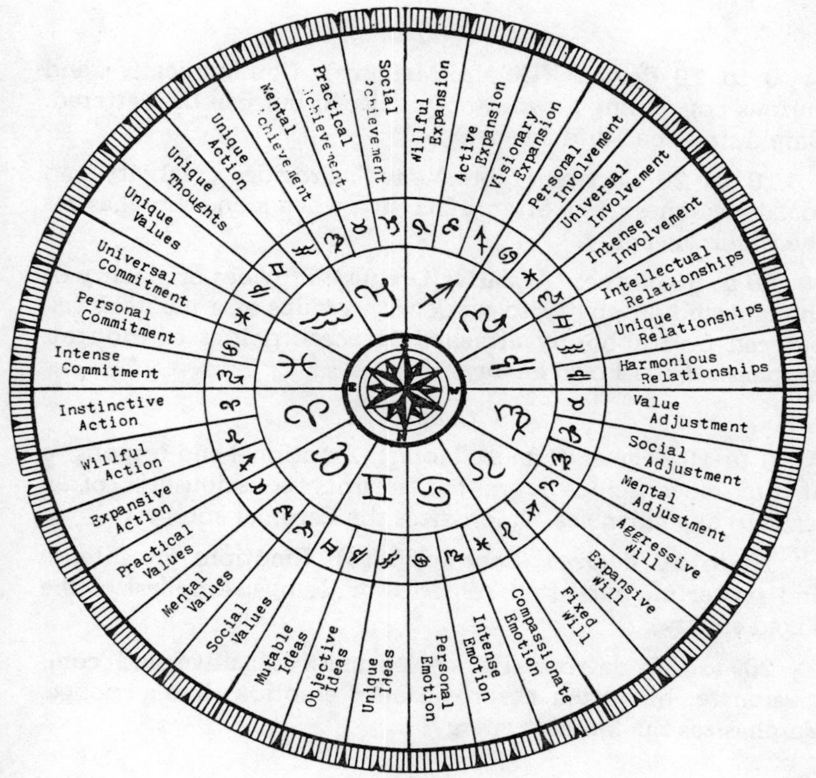

20 to 30 degrees (Sagittarius/Jupiter). Provides optimism and vision, but often restless. Emphasizes the Mutable energy.

Taurus

0 to 10 degrees (Taurus/Venus). Productive and value conscious at the personal level, but can be overly fixed. Emphasizes the Fixed energy.

10 to 20 degrees (Virgo/Mercury). Provides intellectual interests and discrimination of values, but often critical in value expression. Emphasizes the Mutable energy.

20 to 30 degrees (Capricorn/Saturn). Provides strong social ambition, but sometimes overly concerned with prestige. Emphasizes the Cardinal energy.

Gemini

0 to 10 degrees (Gemini/Mercury). Communicative and curious concerning a variety of subjects, but can be scattered. Emphasizes the Mutable energy.

10 to 20 degrees (Libra/Venus). Provides creativity and social awareness, but often indecisive when alone. Emphasizes the Cardinal energy.

20 to 30 degrees (Aquarius/Uranus). Provides originality of thought and an ability to work with groups at a mental level, but can be stubbornly attached to eccentricities of thought. Emphasizes the Fixed energy.

Cancer

0 to 10 degrees (Cancer/Moon). Emotional and responsive at the subconscious level, but security consciousness often leads to dependencies. Emphasizes the Cardinal energy.

10 to 20 degrees (Scorpio/Pluto). Emotions are intense and powerful, but often resentful or jealous. Emphasizes the Fixed energy.

20 to 30 degrees (Pisces/Neptune). Sensitive and compassionate, but often absorbs others' emotions like a sponge. Emphasizes the Mutable energy.

Leo

0 to 10 degrees (Leo/Sun). Dignified, self confident and proud, but sometimes overly ego-centered. Emphasizes the Fixed energy.

10 to 20 degrees (Sagittarius/Jupiter). Provides adaptability and extended vision concerning life goals, but often lacks good judgement. Emphasizes the Mutable energy.

20 to 30 degrees (Aries/Mars). Provides courage and initiative with a need for independence, but can be headstrong and impulsive. Emphasizes the Cardinal energy.

Virgo

0 to 10 degrees (Virgo/Mercury). Analytical and discriminating concerning personal development, but often self-critical. Emphasizes the Mutable energy.

10 to 20 degrees (Capricorn/Saturn). Provides organizing potential and well-defined social goals, but can be overly rigid in ambition. Emphasizes the Cardinal energy.

20 to 30 degrees (Taurus/Venus). Provides sociability and enjoyment of routine, but often lacks initiative. Emphasizes the Fixed energy.

Libra

0 to 10 degrees (Libra/Venus). Concerned with harmony and balance between self and others, but often indecisive when forced to be independent. Emphasizes the Cardinal energy.

10 to 20 degrees (Aquarius/Uranus). Strong mind is stimulated by unique interests, but can be overly detached toward others. Emphasizes the Fixed energy.

20 to 30 degrees (Gemini/Mercury). Adaptable and relates easily to others on a personal level, but often lacks concentrative ability. Emphasizes the Mutable energy.

Scorpio

0 to 10 degrees (Scorpio/Pluto). Intensely emotional while outwardly cool. Experiences the heights and depths of life, but often destructive or controlling while doing so. Emphasizes the Fixed energy.

10 to 20 degrees (Pisces/Neptune). Intense involvement in service to others and aware of spiritual obligations, but sometimes intense involvement with the personal leads to self-destructive actions. Emphasizes the Mutable energy.

20 to 30 degrees (Cancer/Moon). Provides warmth and sympathy when involved, but can be overly self-protective of emotional injury. Emphasizes the Cardinal energy.

Sagittarius

0 to 10 degrees (Sagittarius/Jupiter). Restless urge to expand through larger social participation with others' ideas, but often overly abstract. Emphasizes the Mutable energy.

10 to 20 degrees (Aries/Mars). Provides originality and progressiveness concerning expansion, but often careless. Emphasizes the Cardinal energy.

20 to 30 degrees (Leo/Sun). Provides stability and incorporates personal purpose with expansive activities, but actions can become self-centered. Emphasizes the Fixed energy.

Capricorn

0 to 10 degrees (Capricorn/Saturn). Practical, ambitious and concerned with social respect and accomplishments, but may be overly rigid. Emphasizes the Cardinal energy.

10 to 20 degrees (Taurus/Venus). Softens the harshness of Capricorn while providing strong determination, but sometimes becomes overly demanding. Emphasizes the Fixed energy.

20 to 30 degrees (Virgo/Mercury). Provides potential for organization and quickens the mental processes, but concern for detail often leads to overly critical expectations of self and others. Emphasizes the Mutable energy.

Aquarius

0 to 10 degrees (Aquarius/Uranus). Self-reliant, strongly individualistic and inventive, but often rebellious or erratic in action. Emphasizes the Fixed energy.

10 to 20 degrees (Gemini/Mercury). Increases curiosity concerning the unusual or unknown, but can be superficial or extremely detached. Emphasizes the Mutable energy.

20 to 30 degrees (Libra/Venus). Provides ability to work well with people, using rebellious urges to balance rather than to destroy, but often lacks warmth. Emphasizes the Cardinal energy.

Pisces

0 to 10 degrees (Pisces/Neptune). Separative feelings are dissolved in order to contribute to the larger whole, but sometimes overly idealistic resulting in escapism. Emphasizes the Mutable energy.

10 to 20 degrees (Cancer/Moon). Provides strong sympathetic qualities and nurturing capacity on a social level, but often identifies too strongly with social experiences. Emphasizes the Cardinal energy.

20 to 30 degrees (Scorpio/Pluto). Provides self-control and staying power concerning commitments, but sometimes uses inner strengths to control rather than to contribute. Emphasizes the Fixed energy.

The Nodes

The Nodes of the Moon represent sensitive areas on the ecliptic where the Moon crosses on its pathway around the earth. The North Node represents the point where the Moon crosses the ecliptic moving north, while the South Node (which is always directly opposite from the North) represents the point where the Moon crosses the ecliptic moving south.

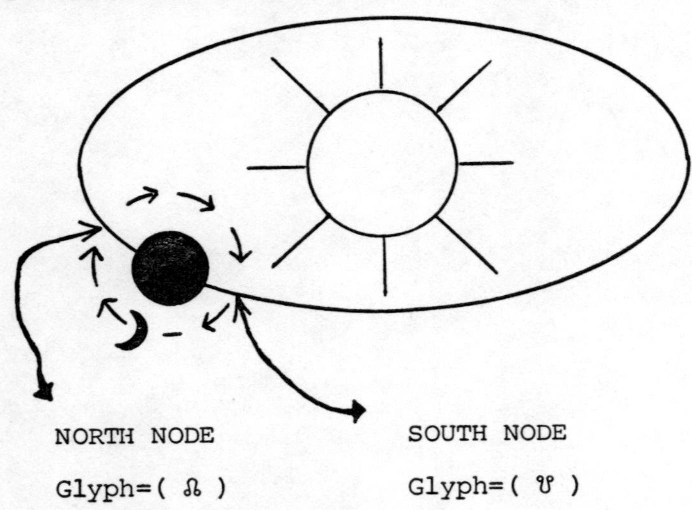

The Nodes point to areas of life (houses) where integration is needed. The North Node describes, by house and sign, where growth is needed. It encourages new experiences which, while not always comfortable or easy, ultimately bring about growth and illumination. The South Node, on the other hand, represents what comes easily or naturally. It shows what you can fall back on when your load gets too heavy, but it can also point to the "easy way out," discouraging growth and encouraging dependency on old habits.

The Nodes are extremely important to consider when interpreting a chart. They show, by their natural opposition, where a balance is needed. Once this balance is found, integration results. To balance this axis in your chart, it is important for you to seek out experiences involving the area of life described by the North Node's house and to develop the qualities of its sign. Then, to express or project what you have learned through your South Node experiences.

As the South Node represents a quality (sign) and a department of life (house) which comes naturally to you, you are encouraged to give something of your talents here so that others can benefit through them. However, in order to keep your contributions meaningful and applicable to the conditions of the moment, you must "feed" yourself through the North Node's activities.

Give and take is the keynote of the Nodes. To give through the South Node without acquiring, absorbing or taking in new experiences through the North Node area of your life results in physical, emotional and spiritual drain. You could find, for example, that people whose Sun sign is the same as your South Node "take" from you, while those whose Sun sign is the same as your North Node have something important to offer even though the latter types of relationships may not be comfortable. Growth seldom is. This does not imply that you should stay away from people having their Sun or other important planets in the same sign as your South Node, but warns you that it could become a draining relationship unless you are consciously working at projects described by your North Node. In essence, those having important planets in the sign of your South Node need something that you have to offer. This, of course, can be a beautiful experience. BUT, it could turn into a one-way relationship if you allow them to take to the point you no longer have the energy to work toward your North Node growth potential.

In my own astrological practice, I place a great deal of emphasis on the Moon's Nodes and I encourage you to use them in all charts that you consider. I feel that the Nodes often show the "key" which helps people put their lives together to work more creatively for themselves as well as those around them.

The Journey Continues

Our journey together has now reached completion. However, as you continue your studies into astrology, you will find that the search for understanding has no real ending. What has been offered in this book is an introduction to the basics of astrology, one step in a journey that has many exciting paths to explore. With a solid foundation beneath you, you are now equipped to take the next step, to explore further the more intricate aspects of the natal chart, to investigate the engrossing realms of transits and progressions, or to discover the more specialized options available to you through this fascinating science of astrology.

As with all journeys, it is important that you are thoroughly prepared for each stage of development along your way. As you begin to interpret charts for friends and clients, you are inviting them to take part in your expedition. Make sure you chart your course carefully, and remember, as pilot, you are responsible for the well-being of your passengers. If you are secure in your knowledge, your journey will lead to fulfillment, not only for yourself, but for all those with whom you share your expertise.

Other Books by the Author

In Search of a Fulfilling Career
Intercepted Signs—Environment Vs. Destiny

Books Co-authored with Jinni Meyer

The Digested Astrologer
When Your Sun Returns
The Spiral of Life

For more information on the above titles, write to:

SEARCH
P. O. Box 162, Northgate Station
Seattle, Washington 98125

NEW TITLES FROM CRCS

A SPIRITUAL APPROACH TO ASTROLOGY by Myrna Lofthus $12.50

THE ASTROLOGER'S GUIDE TO COUNSELING: Astrology's Role in the Helping Professions by Bernard Rosenblum, M.D. ....$ 7.95

THE JUPITER/SATURN CONFERENCE LECTURES by Stephen Arroyo & Liz Greene ....$ 8.95

THE OUTER PLANETS & THEIR CYCLES: The Astrology of the Collective by Liz Greene ....$ 7.95

CHILD SIGNS: Understanding Your Child Through Astrology by Dodie & Allan Edmands ....$ 6.95

DYNAMICS OF ASPECT ANALYSIS: New Perceptions in Astrology by Bil Tierney ....$ 8.95

THE PRACTICE & PROFESSION OF ASTROLOGY: Rebuilding Our Lost Connections with the Cosmos by Stephen Arroyo ....$ 7.95

ASTROLOGY FOR THE NEW AGE: An Intuitive Approach by Marcus Allen ....$ 5.95

CRCS PUBLICATIONS

CRCS PUBLICATIONS publishes high quality books that focus upon the modernization and reformulation of astrology. We specialize in pioneering works dealing with astrological psychology and the synthesis of astrology with counseling and the healing arts. CRCS books utilize the insights of astrology in a practical, constructive way as a tool for self-knowledge and increased awareness.

ASTROLOGY, PSYCHOLOGY & THE FOUR ELEMENTS: An Energy Approach to Astrology & Its Use in the Counseling Arts by Stephen Arroyo
.... $7.95 Paperback; $14.95 Hardcover
An international best-seller, this book deals with the relation of astrology to modern psychology and with the use of astrology as a practical method of understanding one's attunement to universal forces. Clearly shows how to approach astrology with a real understanding of the energies involved. Awarded the British Astrological Assn's. Astrology Prize. A classic translated into 8 languages!

ASTROLOGY AND THE MODERN PSYCHE: An Astrologer Looks at Depth Psychology by Dane Rudhyar .... 182 pages, Paperback $5.95
Deals with Depth-Psychology's pioneers with special emphasis on Jung's concepts related to astrology. Chapters on: Psychodrama, Psychosynthesis, Sex Factors in Personality, the Astrologer's Role as Consultant.

ASTROLOGY, KARMA, & TRANSFORMATION: The Inner Dimensions of the Birth-Chart by Stephen Arroyo .... 264 pages, $9.95 Paperback; $17.95 Deluxe Sewn Hardcover
An insightful book on the use of astrology as a tool for spiritual and psychological growth, seen in the light of the theory of karma and the urge toward self-transformation. International best-seller.

CYCLES OF BECOMING: The Planetary Pattern of Growth by Alexander Ruperti
.... 6 x 9 Paperback, 274 pages, $9.95
The first complete treatment of transits from a humanistic and holistic perspective. All important planetary cycles are correlated with the essential phases of psychological development. A pioneering work!

AN ASTROLOGICAL GUIDE TO SELF-AWARENESS by Donna Cunningham, M.S.W.
.... 210 pages, Paperback $6.95
Written in a lively style by a social worker who uses astrology in counseling, this book includes chapters on transits, houses, interpreting aspects, etc. A popular book translated into 3 languages.

RELATIONSHIPS & LIFE CYCLES: Modern Dimensions of Astrology by Stephen Arroyo
.... 228 pages, Paperback $7.95
A collection of articles and workshops on: natal chart indicators of one's capacity and need for relationship; techniques of chart comparison; using transits practically; counseling; and the use of the houses in chart comparison.

REINCARNATION THROUGH THE ZODIAC by Joan Hodgson ..... Paperback $5.50
A study of the signs of the zodiac from a spiritual perspective, based upon the development of different phases of consciousness through reincarnation. First published in England as *Wisdom in the Stars.*

LOOKING AT ASTROLOGY by Liz Greene .... 8½ x 11, $5.95
A beautiful, full-color children's book for ages 6-13. Illustrated by the author, this is the best explanation of astrology for children and was highly recommended by *School Library Journal.* It emphasizes a healthy self-acceptance and a realistic understanding of others. A beautiful gift for children or for your local library.

STAR SIGNS FOR LOVERS by Liz Greene .... Special Hardcover Value, $7.95
A lively, entertaining, and original discussion of many aspects of the relationship potential of the zodiacal signs. Includes the "shadow" side of the personality, many mythological references, etc.

A SPIRITUAL APPROACH TO ASTROLOGY by Myrna Lofthus ... Paperback $12.50
A complete astrology textbook from a karmic viewpoint, with an especially valuable 130-page section on karmic interpretations of all aspects, including the Ascendant & M.C. A huge 444-page, [illegible] mal work.

THE ASTROLOGER'S GUIDE TO COUNSELING: Astrology's Role in the Helping Professions by Bernard Rosenblum, M.D. .... Paperback $7.95
Establishes astrological counseling as a valid, valuable, and legitimate helping profession, which can also be beneficially used in conjunction with other therapeutic and healing arts.

THE JUPITER/SATURN CONFERENCE LECTURES *(Lectures on Modern Astrology Series)* by Stephen Arroyo & Liz Greene .... Paperback $8.95
Transcribed from lectures given under the 1981 Jupiter Saturn Conjunction, talks included deal with myth, chart synthesis, relationships, & Jungian psychology related to astrology.

THE OUTER PLANETS & THEIR CYCLES: The Astrology of the Collective *(Lectures on Modern Astrology Series)* by Liz Greene .... Paperback $7.95
Deals with the individual's attunement to the outer planets as well as with significant historical and generational trends that correlate to these planetary cycles.

List of Titles Continued on next Page.